PERSONAL FINANCE

ESSENTIALS

Credit
and Borrowing

VOLUME III

PERSONAL FINANCE

ESSENTIALS

Credit
and Borrowing

VOLUME III

JULIA A. HEATH

✔ Facts On File
An Infobase Learning Company

Personal Finance Essentials: Credit and Borrowing

Copyright © 2012 Julia A. Heath

Facts On File, Inc.
An imprint of Infobase Learning
132 West 31st Street
New York NY 10001

Library of Congress Cataloging-in-Publication Data
Heath, Julia A.
  Personal finance essentials / Julia A. Heath.
    v. cm.
  Vol. 2 by Jane S. Lopus.
  Includes bibliographical references and index.
  Contents: v. 1. Decision making and budgeting — v. 2. Education and careers — v. 3. Credit and borrowing — v. 4. Saving and investing.
   ISBN 978-1-60413-986-0 (v. 1 : alk. paper) — ISBN 978-1-60413-987-7 (v. 2 : alk. paper) — ISBN 978-1-60413-988-4 (v. 3 : alk. paper) — ISBN 978-1-60413-989-1 (v. 4 : alk. paper)
  1. Finance, Personal. I. Lopus, Jane S. II. Title.
  HG179.H374 2011
  332.024—dc22
                        2011004564

Facts On File books are available at special discounts when purchased in bulk quantities for businesses, associations, institutions, or sales promotions. Please call our Special Sales Department in New York at (212) 967-8800 or (800) 322-8755.

You can find Facts On File on the World Wide Web at http://www.infobaselearning.com

Text design by Erik Lindstrom
Composition by Erik Lindstrom
Cover printed by IBT Global, Troy, N.Y.
Book printed and bound by IBT Global, Troy, N.Y.
Date printed: December 2011
Printed in the United States of America

10 9 8 7 6 5 4 3 2 1

Contents

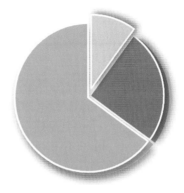

Introduction

What do you think of when you hear the term *financial literacy*? You probably have been hearing it a lot lately. As a result of the recent financial crisis, many people are calling for a greater level of financial literacy in the general population and among students in particular. But what does being "financially literate" mean? According to one popular notion, if someone knows how to write a check and balance his or her checkbook, then he or she is financially literate. Another view holds that someone who knows the benefits of saving is financially literate. These views all certainly reflect aspects of financial literacy, but they do not come close to describing what it really is.

In these volumes, we explore several topics: budgeting, getting an education, saving and investing, using credit wisely. Again, these are all components of what is commonly understood to be financial literacy. But also in these volumes is an emphasis on decision making—which is why it is the subject of the first volume in this series. The ability to make good decisions—identifying the important (and not-so-important) factors that should be considered, being able to weigh your options critically, being aware of the opportunity cost—is a skill that you will use over and over in your life. Being financially literate means that you understand how to make good decisions about money. So while the content of this set is an application of good decision-making skills, we hope that you recognize and apply the broader lessons to the non-financial aspects of your life as well.

When you hear the term *financial literacy*, do you feel excited to learn about it? Or anxious because you do not know anything about it, and you think it will be complicated? Or bored silly? Probably most people would choose the second or third answer—or maybe both. At the same time that there is general agreement that we need more financial literacy, it has gotten a bad rap. Financial literacy is often viewed as very complicated or, worse, extremely boring. It is neither. It just requires a change of perspective.

What if someone forced you to sit in a little box for several minutes each day—maybe for as long as an hour or more? You could not sleep, use your phone, or get up to walk around after a few minutes, you could not even let your mind wander. You would have to stay focused and just sit there. Does that seem like something you would be excited about doing? How excited were you when you learned to drive? When driving is described as it was above, it does not sound like something anyone would want to do. But you probably were very excited to learn to drive—not because of the physical movements associated with driving but because it represents independence and a rite of passage to adulthood. And it gets you from here to there.

The same is true with learning about financial literacy. Going through the mechanics of setting up a budget, a savings plan, investigating your education options, informing yourself so you do not fall victim to scams—none of that is very exciting in and of itself. But what it represents *is* exciting. It represents independence, being in control of your life. It represents a rite of passage—you are responsible for your financial future with the choices you make today. And it gets you from here to there. If you know or have talked to someone who does not have control over their financial lives, you have an idea of how consuming and debilitating the worry associated with that choice can be. The purpose of this set is to give you the skills you need to be purposeful in your decision making and to be able to take control of your life. Wherever your "here" is, with the help of these volumes, you can get to a better "there."

—Julia A. Heath

Credit: History and Importance

In Shakespeare's *Hamlet,* Lord Polonius advises his son, "Neither a borrower nor a lender be; for loan oft loses both itself and friend, and borrowing dulls the edge of husbandry." What Polonius means, of course, is that lending and borrowing between friends often result in the loss of both the funds and the friend. He also warns that getting into a habit of borrowing discourages thrift (husbandry), or living within one's means. More than 400 years later, we do not appear to be heeding Polonius's advice. As of January 2010, total *consumer debt* in the United States was $2.46 trillion. Consumer debt is defined as debt that is not secured by real estate, so this figure does not include *mortgages.* That works out to about $8,100 for every person in the United States: men, women, and children. More sobering, of households with credit card debt (as of March 2010), the size of the debt averages above $8,000,

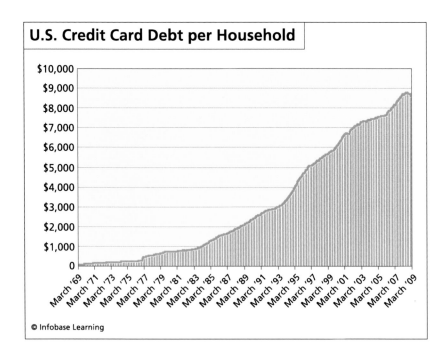

U.S. Credit Card Debt per Household

© Infobase Learning

according to the Federal Reserve. Although it has started to decline recently, the amount of revolving debt owed by consumers has steady increased for most of the past decade.

Clearly, as a nation we have come to rely on borrowing to support our lifestyles. Is this necessarily bad—for both individuals and the country as a whole? Before we examine in detail the various aspects of credit and borrowing, we need to understand the history of credit and how the availability of credit is a factor in our country's overall economic health.

A BRIEF HISTORY OF CREDIT

While credit cards date back only since the 1950s, other forms of credit have been around for quite some time. Beginning in the 1700s, tallymen accepted weekly payments in exchange for clothes. They kept track of credits and payments by carving notches, or "talleys" in a wooden stick. In the early 1900s, some businesses—oil companies and hotels, in particular—issued charge plates to their best customers. These plates could only be used with the business that issued it. Soon other businesses began issuing similar plates to encourage people to buy at their stores and to encourage customer loyalty. Eventually, groups of merchants got together and agreed to accept each other's charge plates as payment for goods and services in their own stores, allowing consumers a wider range of options when shopping.

By the 1920s, buying on credit was quite commonplace. Consumers were buying houses using credit (taking out mortgages), and also taking out loans to buy the latest technological wonder: automobiles. When the Great Depression hit, many merchants still extended credit to their customers who were having a hard time paying for necessities such as groceries and medicines.

The first credit card (a charge plate with wide acceptance) was created by John Briggins in 1946. The "Charge-It" program allowed businesses to deposit the sales slips from credit purchases into their bank accounts at Briggins's bank. The bank would then credit the merchants' accounts, just as if the merchants had deposited cash. The bank, in turn, would bill the merchants' customers for the credit payments. Shortly after the Charge-It program began, Diner's Club offered a card (made out of cardboard) which allowed customers to dine in any of several different restaurants in New York City and be billed later. Both the Charge-It program and the Diner's Club card required that the customer pay their balance in full upon being billed. Therefore, these payment plans are known as *charge cards,* not *credit cards,* which allow customers to pay their balances over time. American Express issued

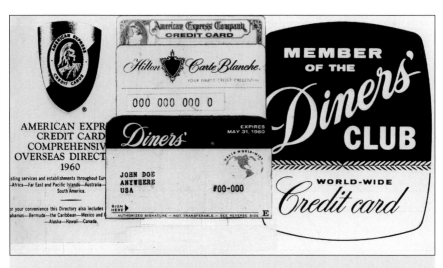

Montage of credit card images, 1960 (*Library of Congress*)

its charge card in the late 1950s, the first card that was made out of plastic.

A true credit card (allowing customers to spread their payments over time) came about a few years later, in the 1960s. Bank of America instituted the BankAmerica Service Corporation, which offered the Visa brand to member banks nationwide. At about the same time, a group of banks that issued credit joined together to form the InterBank Card Association, the forerunner of MasterCard. Both of these organizations offered credit cards through their member banks, requiring a great deal of agreement and cooperation in terms of processing payments and funds transfers. American Express entered the credit card market in 1987, formerly restricting itself to only issuing charge cards. The Discover card appeared on the market through the Sears Corporation in 1986. Up until 2004, both Visa and MasterCard had exclusive arrangements with banks and other card issuers wherein only Visa or MasterCard credit cards could be offered to customers. The federal government charged that this arrangement violated antitrust laws, so now card issuers can offer their customers American Express and Discover cards as well as Visa and MasterCard.

DEBT AND THE ECONOMY

As we have seen, while credit cards are a fairly recent invention, our economy has incorporated credit for quite some time. Indeed, our economy relies on credit and debt to function. Credit agreements lend stability to the economy. Because they are contractual obligations, they add an element of certainty into business transactions. For example, if you sell cars on a cash-only basis, you would have a hard time predicting what your sales volume will be from one week to the next. You never know when people have saved up enough money to buy a car, and you might go weeks without selling any at all. If you sell on credit, however, people sign a contract, obligating them to pay for the car over time. This means that more people will come in to buy cars, but it also means that you are more certain about the cash flow coming into your business. More certainty means you are better able to make plans to hire more people, expand your business and meet your own financial obligations.

The other major benefit of credit in an economy is that borrowing allows consumers to purchase goods and services they would not otherwise be able to afford. Let us say you want to buy a car, but you do not have the entire purchase price of a car saved up. In the absence of credit, you simply would not be able to buy the car until you had saved up the entire cost. With credit, however, you can take out a loan for the balance and buy the car. This is not only good for you, it is good for the economy.

This is how it works. When you buy your car (with borrowed funds), the salesperson who sold you the car earns more money (the commission from the sale), and the dealership must place an order for another car from the factory to replace the one that you bought. The salesperson now has more money to spend on other things, like clothes. The automobile factory now has to increase production to replace the car that you bought, meaning that the automobile workers are earning more money. They will take their extra money and buy other things, such as clothes. The clothing industry will then experience an increase in demand, and its workers will earn more money, which they will use to buy other things, such as toasters. The appliance industry will experience an increase in demand, and so on.

Of course, it is not just *you* buying a new car—lots of people are buying new cars, creating a lot of new income flowing through the economy. This is called the *multiplier effect*. Increases in demand in one sector of the economy can multiply throughout the economy, increasing demand and incomes in many other sectors. The availability of credit greatly facilitates the multiplier effect since it allows consumers to buy goods and services that they would not otherwise be able to afford. Why is this so important to the economy as a whole? Because about two-thirds of our economy is driven by consumer spending (as opposed to spending by businesses or the government). In fact, consumer spending and spending based on credit are so important that when the economy is in a recession, one of the first things that usually happens is that interest rates are lowered to encourage spending and borrowing.

S&P/Case-Shiller Home Prices (Chicago v. New York)

Source: S&P Indices and Fiserv. Data through October 2010

© Infobase Learning

From the discussion above, you might get the idea that the best thing for the country would be for everyone to go deeply in debt in order to spend, spend, spend. Not quite. While consumer spending is a very important component of the economy, taking on huge amounts of debt to finance that spending is very risky for the individual and the country. A large part of the debt that households take on is in the form of home mortgages. As consumers have taken on ever growing levels of debt to finance larger and larger homes, the economy has grown, and so, too, has personal wealth. Individuals' wealth increased because the value of these homes has typically increased, so they own an asset which has *appreciated* (increased) in value. As these homes increase in value, homeowners have an additional opportunity to borrow—they can borrow from the *equity* in their homes (more on home equity loans in chapter 3). Many homeowners borrow on their home equity to finance college educations, vacations, and other large purchases. This situation is sustainable on one condition—that the value of their homes keeps increasing. If instead, the value of their homes falls, these homeowners will find themselves with an asset that is *depreciating* (decreasing in value), and the equity in their homes is decreased or even negative. As other loans become due, they have no other source of borrowed funds. The collapse of the housing market was a major factor in the financial meltdown of 2008–09. Housing prices fell, foreclosures increased and households found themselves owing more on their homes than what they were worth. This eliminated a significant source of potential borrowed funds for households and in some cases, the use of other debt (such as credit cards) increased.

SUMMARY

So some debt is good, but too much is bad. How much is just right? The remainder of this volume will present many of the types of borrowing that consumers have available to them. As we discussed, going into debt in and of itself is not problematic. Indeed, the country could not grow without credit and borrowing. The real concern is that as consumers take on more and more debt, they grow accustomed to living beyond their means and create a way of life that is not sustainable. In particular, credit cards can be a very tempting means for financing a lifestyle that consumers cannot afford. Going into debt, by any means, is a risky undertaking, one that should be undertaken only after heeding Polonius's warning that ". . . borrowing dulls the edge of husbandry."

2

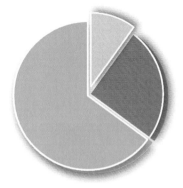

Credit Cards

Do you know someone who has a credit card? The odds are very high that you do. You may even have one yourself. Credit cards have become a part of our culture. You can even pay for your Big Mac with a credit card. Before you take on the responsibility that comes with a credit card, you need to completely understand everything that is involved. There are a lot of terms, rates, loopholes (for the credit card company, not you)—it can all get very confusing. And piling on credit card debt is the easiest way to get into serious trouble. The average credit card balance for college students in 2009, was $3,173, and 21 percent of undergraduates had outstanding balances on their credit cards of between $3,000 and $7,000. Before you get a credit card and find it taking on a life of its own, understand what your obligations and rights are.

A young man shops online with a credit card. The average credit card balance for college students was $3,173 in 2009. (*Shutterstock*)

CREDIT CARD BASICS

When you sign a credit card agreement, you are signing a legal contract. When you use a credit card you are borrowing money from the company that issued the card. Credit cards are the most common example of *revolving debt*. Revolving debt is a loan that does not have a fixed number of payments. Other loans, like car loans or mortgages, have a specified number of payments before the loan is paid off. Revolving debt is "open" in that the amount of the loan varies (increasing when you charge purchases), meaning that the amount of your payments also varies.

Types of Credit Cards

There are actually several different kinds of credit cards. The most common type is the revolving debt type discussed above. You can carry a balance on this type of credit card up to a certain *credit limit,* the maximum amount you can borrow on the card. You can either make monthly payments (there is a required, minimum amount you must pay—the minimum payment) or you can pay off the balance in full each month. If you carry a balance, you will also pay a *finance charge,* the amount you are charged for borrowing the money to carry a balance.

A subgroup of credit cards are *rewards cards.* With rewards cards you get an incentive for using the card. For example, many airlines award frequent flyer miles to users of particular credit cards. The Discover card gives rebates back to customers based on a percentage of total purchases. Other cards have point programs that reward customers with gifts when they accumulate certain point thresholds. In terms of applying for, paying for, and managing these credit cards, they operate the same as standard credit cards.

Store credit cards, or *limited purpose cards,* also operate just like regular credit cards except their use is restricted to a specific store or merchant. Department store credit cards or gas cards are examples of limited purpose cards.

If someone has a bad credit history or is just beginning to establish credit and has trouble qualifying for a regular credit card, a *secured credit card* might be appropriate. All of the credit cards described above issue *unsecured debt,* that is, the debt you accumulate on these cards is not secured by any sort of *collateral.* By contrast, a mortgage is a secured debt. If you fail to pay your mortgage, the bank can foreclose on your home and take possession. The mortgage is secured by the physical asset— the house. When you apply for and use credit card debt, however, there is no physical asset that you are putting up for collateral in the event you fail to pay back the loan. In the case of *default,* the credit card company does not have an asset that it can take back from you to make up for your lack of payment. A secured credit card requires that you make a security deposit (which becomes your credit limit) before you can use the card. Another option for those who are attempting to establish credit is to become an authorized user on someone else's credit card (for example, a parent). A good payment history on such a joint card can help establish a good credit rating, but a poor payment history can work against you.

Recently, a new kind of credit card has appeared, a *contactless credit card.* A contactless credit card does not require you to swipe your card when you purchase something. A special reader just needs to be close to the card and the information is transmitted, allowing you to complete your purchase. Standard credit cards store your information on the magnetic stripe on the back. Contactless credit cards have a magnetic chip that stores data and then transmits it wirelessly to the reader. Some of these new credit cards have the same appearance as standard cards, complete with magnetic stripe so you can use them in the traditional way. Others look like key fobs, particularly those used for convenience stores or some movie theaters. Because these cards never have to leave your hand to be used, credit card companies are claiming that they are safer than the traditional alternative. However, security experts have expressed concern about these cards because the wireless transmissions can be picked up over distances of more than just a few inches, so you are not entirely sure who else could be picking up your information. Credit card companies also claim that the contactless cards allow for quicker transactions since all you do is wave the card in front of the reader (no signature is required). On average, credit card transactions (requiring a signature) take about 25 seconds to complete, while contactless credit card transactions take an average of 15 seconds. The flip side of the advantage in transaction speed, however, is that research studies have shown that consumers use contactless cards more frequently and are likely to spend more than with standard credit cards.

Credit Card Terms

Regardless of the type of credit card, all the information about the card's terms is contained in the information that you receive when you apply for the card: the interest rate you will be charged, how your payments will be computed, when your payments are due, and what will happen if you are late or miss a payment. All too often, this information is ignored when people sign credit card agreements. In fact, 36 percent of cardholders do not know what interest rate their cards carry. So, let us look at the individual components of credit card agreements.

One of the most important aspects of a credit card is the finance charge. If you do not fully pay off your balance each month—if you carry a balance forward to the next month—some rate of interest will be applied to

Front and Back of a Credit Card

1. Issuing bank logo
2. Hologram
3. Credit card number
4. Card brand logo
5. Expiration date
6. Cardholder name
7. Contactless chip
8. Magnetic stripe
9. Signature strip
10. Card security code

© Infobase Learning

this outstanding balance. This is the finance charge—the amount you pay for having a balance. The amount of the finance charge will depend, of course, on the size of the balance you carry forward, but also on two additional pieces of information contained in your credit card agreement: the interest rate and the method used to calculate finance charges.

A credit card actually has several interest rates, all expressed as an *annual percentage rate* (APR). The annual percentage rate is simply the interest rate you are charged for the loan, expressed on a yearly basis. Some credit cards express their interest rates as a monthly rate, but they are also required to express them in yearly terms, as an APR. By requiring all companies (not just credit card companies) to express their interest rates in terms of an APR, it allows the consumer to better compare rates since they are all expressed in the same terms.

A card's APR can be either a *variable* or *fixed rate*. As the name implies, a variable APR changes according to some benchmark interest rate that it is tied to. For example, a credit card's interest rate might be the *prime rate* + 4 percent. The prime rate is the interest rate that banks charge their best customers, and it fluctuates with changes in economic conditions. Following the same logic, you might expect that a fixed APR means that the credit card's interest rate does not change. You would be wrong. A fixed APR is nonchanging only in the sense that the credit card company must give you 45 days notice before it changes it. The notice must be in writing, and you have the option to cancel your card. If you do so, the company must give you five years to pay off your balance. The 45-day notice requirement does not apply to variable rate cards, or if it is a case where an introductory rate expires (see Teaser Rates, below).

Credit card companies can apply this APR to arrive at a finance charge in several different ways. For all of the examples below, assume that your billing period goes from April 1 through April 30. Let us further assume that you carry a balance forward from March of $300. You purchase something on April 15 for $50 and something on April 27 for $30. On April 5, your payment of $100 is received and posted to your account. Your APR is 21 percent, meaning that the monthly interest rate is about 1.8 percent (21/12). Following are some of the ways a credit card company can use to compute the finance charge.

Average Daily Balance. With this method, the credit card company computes what your average daily balance was for the billing period and multiplies that average by approximately 1/12 of your APR to arrive at your finance charge. In our example, the finance charge would be computed as follows:

ACCOUNT ACTIVITY	BALANCES
April 1–April 4 (4 days × $300)	$1,200 (balance from March)
April 5–April 14 (10 days × $200)	$2,000 (payment of $100)
April 15–April 26 (12 days × $250)	$3,000 (purchase of $50)
April 27–April 30 (4 days × $280)	$1,120 (purchase of $30)
Total	$7,320
$7,320/30 (days in the billing period) ; $244 average daily balance	
Finance charge ; $244 × 1.8%; $4.39	

Ending Balance Method.   This method is a much simpler computation. The interest rate is simply applied to the current month's ending balance.

Previous month's ending balance:	$300
Additional charges:	$ 80
Payments:	($100)
Total	$280 Ending balance
Finance charge ; $280 × 1.8%; $5.04	

Previous Balance Method.   This method computes the finance charge on the previous month's balance *before* the current billing period's additional purchases and/or payments are added. For our example, the previous month's balance was $300, so the finance charge for the current billing period (April) would be $300 × 1.8 percent or $5.40. Obviously, if you did not carry a balance forward, you would incur no finance charges in the current period.

Adjusted Balance Method.   This method is the most advantageous for consumers. The finance charge is calculated after the previous month's balance has been reduced by any payments, but before the addition of any new purchases. For our example, the previous month's balance was $300 and a payment was credited of $100. So the finance charge would be $3.60 ($200 × 1.8 percent). The two purchases made in the month would be added to the balance, but would not be used in calculating the finance charge.

Other APRs.   The chances are good that when you look carefully at your credit card offer, you will not see just one

APR. Most credit card companies have several APRs—finance charges are just one of them.

1. Cash Advances. With a credit card you can not only purchase goods and services, but you can also get cash, called *cash advances.* As with all credit card transactions, these are loans and usually carry a much higher APR than purchases do—usually between 2 percent and 4 percent higher. There is no *grace period* with cash advances—you start paying interest the moment you receive the cash. Cash advances also come with fees attached (see below).

2. Teaser Rates. You have probably seen advertisements for a 0 percent credit card. It sounds as if you will not have to pay any finance charges if you use the card and carry a balance, but there is a catch. These low introductory rates are temporary. By law, the *teaser rate* must last at least six months, and you must be told what rate will be in effect after the introductory period is over.

3. Transfer Rates. Similar to teaser rates, *transfer rates* are APRs that will be charged if you transfer a balance from an old credit card to a new one. These are low, designed to bring in new customers. However, sometimes the low APR only applies to the balances that are transferred, not to any new purchases that are made on the new card.

4. Default Rate. If you miss or are late with a payment, your APR might increase. The

new, higher rate is called the *default rate*. The credit card company must disclose what this rate is.

When you pay for a purchase with a credit card, you do not immediately start accumulating interest. The grace period is the number of days you have until interest starts accruing on your balance. Usually a grace period only applies when you have not carried a balance forward from the previous month. If you are carrying a balance forward, interest can start accumulating on your purchases as soon as you make them.

Fees.   Your credit card agreement also spells out a number of fees, starting with the very first contact you have with the credit card company.

1. *Application Fee.* This is the fee that credit card companies charge you to apply for a card. The fee varies by card, but cannot be more than 25 percent of the initial credit limit. Some cards advertise that they do not charge an application fee. Even if a card has an *application fee* attached, sometimes a call to the credit card company will get the fee waived.

2. *Annual Fee.* Most credit card companies charge an *annual fee* for the privilege of having a card. This is not tied to finance charges you might accrue on unpaid balances. This is a fee you pay for having the card, irrespective of whether you use it or not. Rewards cards are more likely to have annual fees than others. As with application fees, the annual fee

cannot be more than 25 percent of the initial credit limit.

3. *Balance Transfer Fee.* If you transfer a balance from an old card to a new card, sometimes the new card will charge you a fee for doing so, usually 1–3 percent of the balance transferred. As discussed above, often the company offers a low *balance transfer* rate of interest, but be aware that any fee for transferring the balance could offset the lower interest rate you will get.

A young woman pays for gasoline with her credit card. One-fourth of the college students surveyed in the U.S. PIRG's 2008 Campus Credit Trap report said that they had paid at least one late fee. (*Shutterstock*)

4. *Cash Advance Fee.* The APR for cash advances is higher than that for purchases and takes effect immediately (no grace period). In addition to this higher APR, the credit card company might also charge a fee for getting a cash advance, like balance transfer fees, usually 1–3 percent of the amount received.

5. *Late Fee.* If you are late with a payment (or do not make one), or your payment is less than the minimum payment required, your APR might increase. In addition, you will be assessed a *late fee.* This fee cannot be more than your minimum payment, with a maximum fee of $25. Even if your payment is on time, it could be late. Credit card companies are required by law to credit payments the day they are received. But, some credit card companies have very specific rules about how payments are to be sent in and what address is to be used when mailing a payment. If any of their rules are violated, the company can take up to five days to credit the payment, possibly making your "on-time" payment, late.

6. *Over-the-Limit Fee.* If you have a balance on your card that is greater than the credit limit the company allowed you, you will be charged an over-the-limit fee. This fee cannot be more than the amount of the overage, and will be assessed each billing cycle you are over your credit limit. You may wonder how you could go over your credit limit— does not the credit card company disallow purchases that would send you over the

limit? Not unless you tell them to. Called "opting in," it means that you tell your credit card company that you want them to cover charges that are over your credit limit. Opting in comes with a high price tag—the fee described above. If you choose to opt in, be aware that over-the-limit fees can be difficult to get rid of. For example, if you transfer a credit card balance from an old card to a new card and the new card has a credit limit that is lower than the balance you are transferring, you will be assessed an over-the-limit fee immediately. For example, let us assume you have a balance on a card of $1,000. You want to transfer that balance to a new card (the interest rate is lower), but the new card has a credit limit of $800. As soon as you transfer your old balance of $1,000 to the new card, you will be assessed an over-the-limit fee.

In addition, over-the-limit fees are assessed on the balance of your account, not just the purchases. If you are carrying a balance, for example, and that balance is close to, but not over the credit limit, you still may be assessed an over-the-limit fee. How? When your finance charge is added to your balance, it may put your balance over your limit. The addition of late fees can have the same outcome. For example, assume your balance on your credit card is $989, and your credit limit is $1,000. You send in a payment of $50, so you have nothing to worry about, right? Except your payment was received a day late, so you now have incurred a late fee of $39, which puts your balance over your credit limit, meaning you have also incurred an over-the-limit fee of $39. The easiest way to avoid over-the-limit fees is to not opt in, to not authorize the credit card company to allow you to go over your limit.

7. *Foreign transaction fee.* If you travel abroad and use your credit card, you may be assessed a 1–3 percent *foreign transaction fee* on each purchase. You also may be charged a *currency exchange fee.*

As is obvious from the extensive discussion above, there are several factors that you should be aware of before signing the credit card agreement. The various interest rates, the computation of finance charges, the fees—all of these factors must be spelled out in detail in the credit card agreement and be made known to you before you sign the contract.

MANAGING YOUR CREDIT CARD
Monthly Statements

Once you have your credit card, you will begin receiving monthly statements of your account. While each issuer's statement looks different, they are all required to contain certain information. All the numbers can make statements look a bit intimidating, but when each line is broken down they make a lot more sense. It is very important that you understand and check your statement every month to make sure there are no errors. An uncorrected error can cost you both money and points on your credit score.

Let us look at the sample statement below. This is the summary page of a typical statement.

Credit Card Statement

Payment information

New Balance Total...$897.30
Current Payment Due...$15.00
_____
Total Minimum Payment Due................................$15.00
Payment Due Date...4/12/10

Late Payment Warning: If we do not receive your minimum payment by the date listed above, you may have to pay a late fee of up to $39.00.

Minimum Payment Warning: If you make only the minimum payment each period, you will pay more in interest and it will take you longer to pay off your balance. For example:

If you make no additional charges using this card and each month you pay	You will pay off the balance shown on this statement in about	And you will end up paying an estimated total of
Only the minimum payment	7 years	$1,249.23
$28.91	36 months	$1,040.76 (Savings= $208.47)

If you would like information about credit counseling services, call 1-866-300-5238.

Account Summary

Previous Balance............................$0.00
Payments and Other Credits.........$0.00
Purchases and Adjustments.......$897.30
Fees Charged...................................$0.00
Interest Charged............................$0.00
_____
New Balance Total....................$897.30

Credit Line.............................$10,000.00
Credit Available......................$9,102.70
Statement Closing Date..............3/16/10

© Infobase Learning

Look at the column at the far right, labeled Account Summary:

- Previous Balance. *Previous balance* is the amount you did not pay off in the previous month and so was carried forward to this month. In this example, there is no balance to carry forward. Always make sure this amount is consistent with your records.

- Payments and Other Credits. This is the line that reflects your payment of last month, as well as any merchandise returns you have made. If you bought something with your credit card and later returned it in this billing cycle, it should show up as a credit to your account on this line. Payments on any cash advances will also show up on this line. Make sure the credit card company has correctly applied any payments.

- Purchases and Adjustments. This line lists your total of the purchases and cash advances for the billing period. It is a good practice to save all your credit card receipts until you get your monthly statement. You can then make sure that you are not being double-billed or billed for something you did not purchase. Purchases are generally itemized on the second page of the statement, allowing you to catch mistakes easily. In the example above, there was a total of $897.30 in new activity on the card this period.

- The next two lines indicate the assessment of any fees or finance charges. The line for fees would reflect such things as late fees, cash advance fees, or balance transfer fees. The next line, interest charged, reflects the application of the APR to the balance carried forward from the previous month. Since there was no balance carried forward in our example, this line is zero.

- New Balance Total. This is arrived at by adding up the previous balance, new purchases, fees and interest, then subtracting any payments.

- Credit Line (or Limit). In our example, the credit limit is $10,000. Remember that this does not mean that $10,000 worth of merchandise can be purchased. The credit limit includes finance charges, fees, and cash advances. So if you purchase $9,910 worth of merchandise, but you have finance charges and late fees that add up to $110, you are over your credit limit and will be assessed an over-the-limit fee. It is better to think of the credit limit as applying to activity, rather than just purchases. Because the current statement balance is $897.30, the amount of activity remaining on this account is $10,000 minus the $897.30, or $9,102.70.

- The next two lines indicate when this billing cycle ended and how many days were in it.

Moving to the left column, we see that the New Balance Total is repeated, followed by the minimum payment required. The due date is also listed. This is the date when your payment must be received by the company. It is not the date that your payment must be postmarked. With the Credit CARD Reform Act of 2009, credit card companies are required to tell you what will happen if your payment is late. They are also required to tell you how long it will take you to pay off your balance and what the total interest payment will be if you only pay the minimum (more on paying the minimum, below). The credit card company must also include information that tells you how much you would need to pay each month in order to pay off the balance in three years.

Minimum Payments

When you charge purchases or get cash advances with a credit card you do not have to pay off the entire amount due every month (as opposed to a charge card that requires full payment each month). In fact, you can pay any amount on your balance, from the full amount down to a minimum payment set by the credit card company. This minimum payment is typically computed as 3–4 percent of your outstanding balance and, as discussed in the section above, the credit card company must give you information on how long it will take to pay off the balance if you only pay that minimum amount. In our example above, the balance was $897.30 with a minimum payment of $15. The table provided on the statement indicates that if no further charges were put on the card and only the minimum payment was made each month, it would take almost 7 years to pay off the $897.30 balance. But paying $15 per month on a $897.30 balance is about 60 months, or 5 years ($897.30/$15), not 7 years. How does 5 years become 7?

The short answer is that every month that you carry a balance forward is a month that you are charged interest on the balance. When the credit card company receives your payment, it does not apply it all to the principle—most of it goes toward interest. Let us go back to our example and see how the credit card company allocates each payment it receives. The balance on the card is $897.30, the minimum payment is $15 and the interest rate is 18 percent. This means that per month, the interest rate is approximately 1.5 percent (18 percent/12 months in a year = 1.5). Therefore, the interest payment the first month is $13.46 (1.5 percent × $897.30). Since the total payment was $15, that only leaves $1.54 left to be applied to the principle, the amount that is owed ($15 – $13.46). The balance for the next month will be the original balance of $897.30 less the amount of the payment that is applied to principle ($1.54), leaving a balance that carries forward of $895.76 ($897.30 – $1.54). The transactions for a year would look like this:

PAYMENT	BALANCE	PAYMENT	AMT. APPLIED TO INTEREST	AMT. APPLIED TO PRINCIPLE	NEW BALANCE
1	$897.30	$15	$13.46	$1.54	$895.76
2	895.76	15	13.44	1.56	894.20
3	894.20	15	13.41	1.59	892.61
4	892.61	15	13.39	1.61	891.00
5	891.00	15	13.37	1.63	889.37
6	889.37	15	13.34	1.66	887.71
7	887.71	15	13.32	1.68	886.03
8	886.03	15	13.29	1.71	884.32
9	884.32	15	13.26	1.74	882.58
10	882.58	15	13.24	1.76	880.82
11	880.82	15	13.21	1.79	879.03
12	879.03	15	13.19	1.81	877.22
	Total	$180			

Notice what is happening on this account. At the end of a year of making payments, the balance on this card is still $877.22. The amount of money that has been paid into the account is $180, but the amount still owed has only decreased by about $20! Remember, no additional purchases or cash advances have been made on the card.

Now let us look at what happens to the same account when more than the minimum payment is made. Let us assume that instead of the $15 minimum payment, you make a payment each of month of $50. Here is what the first year of the account would look like:

PAYMENT	BALANCE	PAYMENT	AMT. APPLIED TO INTEREST	AMT. APPLIED TO PRINCIPLE	NEW BALANCE
1	$897.30	$50	$13.46	$36.54	$895.76
2	860.76	50	12.91	37.09	786.58
3	786.58	50	11.80	38.20	748.38
4	748.38	50	11.23	38.77	709.61
5	709.61	50	10.64	39.36	670.25
6	670.25	50	10.05	39.95	630.30
7	630.30	50	9.45	40.55	589.75
8	589.75	50	8.85	41.15	548.60
9	548.60	50	8.23	41.77	506.83
10	506.83	50	7.60	42.40	464.43
11	464.43	50	6.97	43.03	421.40
12	421.40	50	6.32	43.68	377.72
	Total	$600			

Making a monthly payment of $50 instead of $15 means that in the course of a year, you have paid $600 instead of $180—$420 more. But, your balance is only $377.72, not $877.22 as it would be with a $15 payment. So, by spending $420 more in payments, you have saved almost $500 ($877.22 – $377.72 = $499.50).

If you need some motivation to send in more than the minimum payment on credit card debt, go to www.TheRealDamage.com. This Web site will compute what it would cost to pay off current balances, but also demonstrates the true cost of a new purchase. For example, if you are thinking of spending $50 to buy something, enter that amount in this Web site, and you will learn the true "damage" of the purchase—in other words, what you give up if you spend that money instead of sending it in toward your card balance. You may recognize this concept as opportunity cost from the Decision-Making book.

How-to's

There are several issues that you need manage when you have a credit card beyond being able to read your statement and making payments. This section covers these issues, beginning with what to do when you find yourself without your card.

Lost or Stolen Card. When your credit card has been lost or stolen, your first priority is to contact the credit card company immediately to report it. All major credit card companies have toll-free, 24-hour numbers so you do not need to wait until business hours to report the theft or loss. The company will want to know your account number and other information that you provided when you activated the card, so make sure you keep that information in a safe location, separate from your card.

Be aware that when you report a lost or stolen card, your account is immediately deactivated. If you have simply misplaced your card, later find it, and then attempt to reinstate your account, you will not be able to. If you do later find your card, you should destroy it. Cancelling your card is a nonreversible act. You should follow up the phone call with a letter with the same information. Once you have cancelled your card, you should receive a replacement card with a different account number within a week.

Your financial liability on lost or stolen credit cards once you report them missing is zero. If your card is used before you can report it missing or stolen, your liability is limited to $50 by federal law, no matter how much is charged to the card. If you report the loss quickly, many credit card companies will waive that $50, and you will not be responsible for any of the unauthorized charges. You should check your monthly statements carefully for the next few months to make sure that no unauthorized charges are being posted. If they are, contact your credit card company immediately.

Cancelling a Card.   If you ever want to cancel your credit card (for reasons other than loss or theft), the first thing you need to do is to pay off your balance in full. The next step is to contact your credit card company's customer service department (the toll-free numbers are listed on the card), verify that your balance is zero, then inform them that you want to cancel your card. It is very important that you *not* notify the company that you want to cancel the card before you pay off the balance. Doing so could result in the company raising your interest rate to the highest rate as a penalty. Chances are good that when you tell your company that you want to cancel the card, they will try to convince you not to. They may try very hard to convince you, offering a lower interest rate or other inducements. You may find it worth your while to stay with the company after listening to these pitches, but if you still want to cancel be sure the company is clear about your wishes.

Follow up this phone call with a written letter to the credit card company with the same information that you provided in the call. Finally, check your credit report to make sure that it reflects the cancellation of your card (more on credit reports in chapter 4).

Disputing a Purchase.   When you use your credit card to make a purchase and the product is defective or otherwise not acceptable, or you feel that you have been defrauded by a merchant, you are protected under the Fair Credit Billing Act. Under this federal law, you are entitled to withhold payment from a merchant because of damaged goods or goods that are not the quality you expected. You must make an effort with the merchant to resolve any disputes, but if that effort fails, you can ask the credit card company to withhold payment. Make sure you document your attempt at resolution (dates and names of those you have talked to). If your dispute is still not resolved, write the merchant a letter outlining the problem. Keep a copy of the letter for your records. Your next step is to contact the credit card company, in writing and within 60 days of receipt of the bill with the disputed charge. Send the documentation to the company, including the letter of complaint you sent to the merchant.

The credit card company will contact the merchant and make a determination as to whether your complaint is valid. If they agree with you, you do not owe anything for the disputed purchase. If they agree with the merchant, you will have to pay the disputed amount, plus any finance charges that may have accrued.

Transferring Balances. If you have received a credit card solicitation that offers a low interest rate on a balance you transfer to it from an old card, you need to make sure that you have read and fully understand the agreement. Just because a credit card offer mentions a very low rate it does not mean that you will get that rate, even if it says you are preapproved at that rate. You also need to understand what the credit limit on the new card is (so you do not transfer in a balance that is higher than—

or even close to—that limit). You should be fully aware of what the interest rate on the transferred balance is and verify that it is applied only to the transferred amount, not any new purchases made with the card. Sometimes consumers assume that the low rate applies to new purchases made with the card—that is usually not the case. Make sure you understand what fees are involved in transferring balances. Not all credit card companies charge transfer fees, but of those that do, it is usually the case that the fee is higher the larger the amount transferred. Sometimes the transfer can take a few weeks, so do not neglect to continue to pay on the old card until you get notification that the transfer is complete. Once you receive the notification, verify it with your old credit card company, then cancel the card.

Choosing a Credit Card

With the bewildering array of credit cards, interest rates, annual fees, and rewards, it can be extremely confusing to try and sort it all out and decide which card is right for you. The first step in picking a credit card that will be a good fit for you is to know how you will use it. Will you pay the balance off every month? If so, getting a card that offers rewards might be a good option. Sometimes these cards carry a higher interest rate, but if you are not carrying a balance forward, the higher interest rate does not matter. Are you going to use the card very infrequently, just for emergencies? If so, getting a card with a high annual fee does not make sense. Look for one with a low, or even no annual fee. This is a good practice in all cases, but particularly if you will rarely use your card. Why pay a premium fee for something you only use once a year?

Half of college undergraduates had four or more credit cards in 2008. (*Shutterstock*)

THE CREDIT CARD ACT OF 2009

The Credit Card Accountability, Responsibility and Disclosure [CARD] Act of 2009, is designed to protect consumers against sudden interest rate changes, abusive fees, and other practices that have harmed consumers. While this sweeping reform addresses many of the most common consumer complaints against the credit card industry, it does not address all of them. In this section, we will discuss what new protections exist under this legislation and what practices are not covered that you should be aware of.

What's Covered

1. *Interest Rate Increases.* The credit card company cannot increase your APR on your balance for one year from when you first opened your account, unless:

   a. they told you when you opened the account that the APR would be increased sooner than a year; or
   b. you have a variable APR that is tied to some external measure, like the prime rate, that the credit card company has no control over; or
   c. you are in the middle of a debt reduction program with the credit card company, and you have not fulfilled your requirements; or
   d. you have not made your minimum payment for the past 60 days.

After the first year you have your card, the company can raise your interest rate (or change annual or late fees), but

   a. they have to give you 45 days notice (the old requirement was 15 days).
   b. they must give you the right to cancel your card before the new rate takes effect. If you decide to cancel, the finance charges on your balance will be at the old rate, and you are not required to immediately pay off that balance (you have five years).

c. the higher interest rate only applies to new purchases, not any balance you are carrying forward.

d. the higher rate cannot be greater than the penalty rate that was disclosed in the original credit card agreement.

e. the company has to reassess the reasons for the interest rate increase every six months to make sure that the risk factors that led to the increase are still present. If the review indicates that the rate increase is no longer justified, the credit card company must lower the APR on future transactions. If the company feels that the rate increase is still warranted, it must provide you with a written explanation of their reasons for your rate increase.

If you accept a credit card offer that has a teaser rate, that rate must remain in effect for at least six months after you open your account.

2. *Fee and Interest Charge Limits.* The credit card company must mail you your statement at least 21 days before your payment is due (the old requirement was 14 days). Sometimes credit cards have different interest rates. For example, if you transferred a balance from an old card to a new one and then made additional purchases on your new one, chances are that different interest rates apply to the transferred balance and to your new purchases. In the absence of legislation,

when you would send in a payment, the credit card company would apply that payment to the balance with the *lowest* interest rate (probably the transferred balance). The result is that you pay more interest charges. The new law stipulates that your payment (the amount over the minimum) must first be applied to those balances carrying the *highest* interest rate, allowing you to pay down the most expensive balances more quickly.

In addition, the way your finance charges are computed has changed. Many credit card companies used to engage in *double-cycle billing.* When computing the finance charges on balances, the company would not only use the current billing period's balance, but it also used the average daily balance from the previous cycle, even if you paid a portion of that balance before the current cycle. This is a very expensive practice and is banned under the new Credit CARD Act.

Your credit card company can no longer assess fees (annual fee or application fee) that total more than 25 percent of your credit limit. For example, if your initial credit limit is $1,000, the fees for the first year cannot exceed $250. Fees such as over-the-limit fees or late fees are not included in this restriction.

3. *Disclosures.* Credit card companies must fully disclose not only what the minimum payment due is, but how long it will take to pay off your balance if you only make

the minimum payment and how much you will pay in interest charges. They must also disclose how much your payment must be in order to pay off your balance in 36 months. The payment due date must be prominently displayed, along with the late fee that will accrue if payment is not received by that date. This due date must be the same for every billing cycle, rather than changing from one month to the next. Credit card companies must accept payments received by 5 P.M. on the due date, rather than instituting early morning deadlines that result in late fees for consumer whose payments arrived on the correct date, but later in the day. If your due date falls on a weekend or holiday, you have until the next business day to get your payment in. Credit card companies may no longer assess an over-the-limit fee if you go over your credit limit unless you "opt in" and allow the company to accept transactions that would put you over the limit. If you choose to opt in and go over your limit, the company can only assess a fee one time in the billing cycle, not once for every transaction that puts you over the limit. If you do not opt in and your credit card company allows a transaction to go through that would put you over your limit, you cannot be charged a fee—that is their mistake.

Finally, if you are under the age of 21 you cannot receive a credit card unless the application is cosigned by someone over

21, or you can provide written documentation that you are able to make payments on your account. In addition, credit card companies may not send you "pre-approved" solicitations unless you have agreed to receive them.

What's Not Covered

As sweeping and consumer-friendly as the Credit CARD Act is, there are significant areas of exposure that remain for credit card users. Since credit card companies have been restricted in some activities, they have looked for other ways to raise revenues.

1. *Interest Rates.* Because the new law restricts credit card companies' ability to change "fixed" rates, most new cards now carry a variable interest rate. As we have seen, the credit card company arrives at the interest rate it charges you by adding a fixed amount to some index or the prime rate. Before the changes in the law, companies used the prime rate as of a specific date, which is spelled out in the agreement. With the new legislation, the language of many credit card contracts specifies that the variable rate will be based on the maximum prime rate for the previous 90 days, resulting in higher variable rates. For example, if the prime rate on the last day of the billing cycle was 3.6 percent, the variable rate you would pay is 3.6 percent plus some fixed amount, say 4 percent, for a total rate of 7.6 percent. Although the prime on the last day was 3.6 percent, the prime

might have been as high as 4 percent during the previous 90 days. If the language in the credit card contract specifies the latter calculation, the interest rate you would pay would be 4 percent plus the fixed amount of 4 percent, for 8 percent.

Remember when we discovered that a "fixed" rate was not really fixed? Now we learn that "variable" does not really mean variable, either—at least not totally. When credit card companies specify how they will compute the variable rate they charge you, the language details how the rate will increase. Implicit in this language is the fact that the variable rate will never decrease from the starting rate. The rate can always go up, but will never fall below the initial rate.

Credit card companies have minimum finance charges, which have been increasing in recent years. For example, if you carry a small balance forward, your finance charge may be very low, say 50 cents. If your credit card has a minimum finance charge of $2.00, however, you will be assessed $2.00, not 50 cents.

2. *Fees.* Several years ago, credit cards instituted a tiered structure for late fees. If you were late with your payment and your balance was low (for example, below $150), you were charged a smaller late fee than if your balance was high (for example, over $1,500). While companies still typically use three tiers, the threshold amounts for each tier have been lowered, so that the highest late

fee kicks in at a lower balance ($250 rather than $1,500).

The Credit CARD Act does not cover inactivity fees, which can be assessed on your account if you have no activity on an open account for some period of time. Some credit card companies have also started assessing account management fees on closed accounts that still have a balance. Why would a closed account have a balance? Remember the new requirements that require that credit card companies give you the opportunity to close your account if you do not like new terms, such as interest rate changes? If you decide to terminate your contract with the company and you still have a balance, you may also be required to pay an inactivity fee while you are paying off the balance.

We have already discussed the international fees that are assessed when you use your credit card in foreign countries. These fees include a fee for the transaction, plus a fee for currency exchange. With the passage of the Credit CARD Act, credit card companies have increased these fees, as well as expanded the definition of international transactions. Fees can now be assessed on internet purchases from merchants who are based in foreign countries, even though they accept dollars as payment.

Credit card companies have raised minimum fees such as those for cash advances, and raised maximum fees for balance transfers. Let us assume that before the Credit

CARD Act took effect, your credit card had a cash advance fee that was equal to 20 percent of the amount advanced. If you took out a $100 advance, your fee would be $20. Let us further assume that after the new legislation took effect, your credit card company instituted a $20 minimum cash advance fee, plus the normal 20 percent fee—your fee is now $40. If you need the $100 cash advance for only one month, your effective annual interest rate on this $100 is 260 percent (12 months × 20 percent = 240 percent + 20 percent—the minimum fee).

SUMMARY

Credit cards—they are everywhere. They can make life much easier. They can help establish a good credit history, accumulate points for your next vacation or give you cash back. They can also be a fast ride to significant debt, a low credit score, and sleepless nights. The new Credit CARD Act includes many consumer protections, but does not eliminate all of the ambiguity and complexity involved in getting a credit card. When you apply for a credit card, you are applying for a loan. After this chapter, you should be better equipped to understand what the credit card contract is saying.

This is a summary of the terms you should look for and make sure you understand before you sign any credit card agreement:

Interest Rates:
    APR—fixed/variable
    Finance Charges
    Cash Advance

    Default Rate

    Teaser Rate

    Transfer Rate

Fees:

    Application

    Annual

    Balance Transfer

    Cash Advance

    Late

    Over-the-Limit

    Foreign Transaction

Grace Period

Credit Limit

Opt-In

Minimum Payment

3

Common Consumer Loans

It is hard to imagine how someone in our economy could manage to completely avoid all forms of consumer debt. In the previous chapter, we talked about credit cards, one of the most common forms of debt. While credit cards are appropriate for many goods and services, there are some purchases that require other forms of loans. This chapter discusses the most common of these consumer loans.

TYPES OF CONSUMER LOANS

While there are many different kinds of consumer loans, they all fall into two broad categories: secured and unsecured. A secured loan is one that is backed up by some asset, called collateral, in case of default. For example, when you take out a car loan, if you fail to pay on the loan, the car will be repossessed. Your loan is secured by the car. Because these loans are backed up by collateral, they are less risky to the lender, and the interest rate is likely to be lower than is the case with an unsecured loan. As you might suspect, an unsecured loan is one in which there is no collateral backing up the loan—a financial institution is willing to loan you money with no asset to secure it. Purchasing merchandise with a credit card is an example of an unsecured loan. These loans are riskier since there is no asset the lender can take back in case of nonpayment, so the interest rate is generally higher.

Consumers need to borrow money for a wide variety of reasons. As we discussed in chapter 1, if credit were not available, consumers would not be able to buy things such as houses, cars, and many household furnishings. We will take a look at the most common of these loans, beginning with car loans.

Car Loans

When you buy a new or used car from a dealership, the chances are good that you will need to finance all or part of the purchase price. You have three choices. You can get a car loan from your financial institution, you can get an online auto loan, or you can get financing from the dealership. Regardless of where you get your auto loan, be aware that you do not own the car after you "buy" it. It is a common misconception that when you sign the loan contract and drive off the car lot, that you are a car owner. You are not. The owner of the car is whatever institution loaned you the money for the car. They are just letting you use the car. Each time you make a monthly payment, you own a little bit more of the car, but it is not totally yours (you do not get the title) until you have made your last payment. Therefore, a car loan is an example of a se-cured loan.

Regardless of where you ultimately borrow the money from, the first step in securing an auto loan is to get both your credit report and your credit score. Credit reports and scores are discussed in detail in chapter 4, but for our purposes in this chapter, you need to know that your credit score is an indicator to financial institutions of what kind of credit risk you are. The higher your score, the better (the maximum score is 850), because high credit scores translate into lower interest rates.

It is impossible to overstate how important this first step is. When you apply for an auto loan from any source, you should be armed with as much information as possible, and no piece of information is more crucial than your credit score. You should also get a copy of your credit report to make sure that all the information that appears on the report is correct. Inaccurate or incomplete information can lower your score, so you need to check your report carefully and contact the credit reporting bureaus if you find errors or omissions. It can take the bureaus up to 30 days to fix information, so you need to plan ahead. You are entitled to one free copy of your credit report per year, but you will have to pay for your credit score. There are three credit reporting bureaus (see bureaus and contact information at the end of the chapter), and you should get a report from each one to make sure all information is accurate. If you discover that your credit score is low (less than 550), you might want to reconsider buying a car for the time being. You will save money if you can increase your credit score and get a lower rate. You can do this by paying off (or reducing) credit card debt and paying your bills on time. You can check your score in another six to nine months to see if your credit score has improved.

A young woman buys a new car. According to the Federal Reserve, the average new car loan in 2009 was more than $28,000. (*Shutterstock*)

Once you have checked your credit score and report, you are ready to do some comparison shopping for loans. Presumably, you already have an idea of the kind of car you are in the market for and an estimate of what that car will cost. Before you ever go to the car dealer you should find out what terms are offered by some financial institutions. Check out your own financial institution and/or a credit union to see what auto loans they offer. Fill out applications and get preapproved for an amount that will cover the cost of the car you are interested in.

Next, research some online institutions that offer auto loans. Often the interest rates offered by online lenders are lower than those you can find elsewhere, and you can get approved in a matter of minutes.

Once you have information from three or more lending institutions and have a preapproval from at least one of them, you are ready to go to the car dealership. The dealership may very well offer you a loan as well, which is convenient, but is usually more expensive than other loans you could qualify for. There are several things to be aware of when you talk to the dealer about financing your car with them.

1. Car dealers will often adjust the terms of the loan to meet your monthly payment requirements, so do not tell them what those monthly requirements are. You may be able to afford the resulting loan on a monthly basis, but it may end up costing you more over the life of the loan than some of the other loans you have researched.

2. Make sure the dealer is using your correct credit score. Sometimes dealers will use an "alternative" credit bureau to generate a lower credit score than the major three credit reporting bureaus do. Be aware that the only purpose of using a bureau other than the "Big 3" is to convince you that the higher interest rate they want to charge you is justified. It is at this point that you can pull out your credit score and show what your true score is. If they will not accept that score (and lower your interest rate), leave.

3. Make sure you check all their numbers by plugging their figures into an auto loan calculator yourself. You can find several online:

Online Car Loan Calculators

http://www.cars.com/go/advice/financing/calc/loanCalc.jsp?mode=full

http://www.edmunds.com/apps/calc/CalculatorController

http://www.bankrate.com/calculators/auto/auto-loan-calculator.aspx.

http://www.onlineloancalculator.org/

4. Try to make at least a 20 percent down payment. Putting a larger amount toward the purchase price up front can save you a lot in interest charges over the life of your loan. You can put in different down payment amounts with the calculators, above, to see the effect on your monthly payment and total cost.

5. Find out if the financing for your car will come from a manufacturer's finance division or if the dealer sells your loan to a third party. The interest rate is likely to be higher in the latter case.

6. Be aware that when you complete the paperwork on your car loan and drive the car off the lot, it still does not mean that the car is yours. There is a clause in car loan contracts that says "Subject to Financing." Sometimes dealers will call a few days later to tell you that your loan fell through. They usually do this in an effort to get more money from you.

This is why it is in your best interest to not go into the dealer until you have a preapproval in your pocket.

7. If you are trading in a car to help finance your new one, make sure you own the car free and clear. If you trade in a car that you still owe money on, the dealer may not pay off your old car in the time frame that was promised. The result? You are on the hook for not only your new car payments, but your old one as well. Until the dealer pays off your old car loan, it is still in your name. If you do trade in a car you still owe money on, be sure you get their commitment in writing to pay off your car within a specified period.

8. If the car dealer offers you a loan with a lower APR than the other offers you have lined up, make sure you are comparing apples to apples. When comparing loans, make sure that the loans are for the same amounts and for the same term, that is, length of the loan. Often dealers will offer a loan with a lower APR, but the length of the loan will be much longer than other offers you have. The good news about longer-term loans is that your monthly payments will be lower. The bad news is that you will end up paying more total interest than if the term of the loan had been shorter. For example, let us assume that you finance $15,000 at 8 percent. If you finance this loan for four years, your monthly payment will be $366.19, and you will pay $2,577.30 in interest over the life of the loan. Instead, if you choose to finance

over six years, your monthly payment will drop to $263.00, but you will pay $3,935.90 in total interest. The other bad news with longer term loans is that you will stay "upside down" on your car for a longer period of time. Being upside down on a loan means that you owe more than the asset is worth. Cars, in particular, lose a lot of their value as soon as drive them off the lot. It is not unusual to owe more than your car is worth for the first two years of a loan. With longer term loans, you can stay upside down longer because the amount of your monthly payment that is going toward reducing the principal is smaller than with a shorter term loan, so your car's value is falling faster than your equity in your car is increasing. If you trade in your car for another one before it is paid off, you risk repeating (if not worsening) this cycle on your next car as well.

9. Have you seen dealers advertising low interest rates (as low as 0 percent)? Sounds like a great deal, right? Be aware that just because dealers advertise low rates, it does not mean that you will actually get them. These low rates are reserved for those customers with the best credit. In fact, only about 10 percent of auto customers walk away with a 0 percent interest rate deal. Even if you do qualify for one of these low rate loans, be aware that the term of the loan is usually very short—12 to 36 months—and they apply only to new car loans. So, if you are in the market for a used car, or if you were planning on a longer term

for your car loan, these low rates are not for you.

But let us assume that you are ready for a new car, you can get the low rate financing for up to 60 months, and that your credit score is good enough to qualify you for a low rate loan. Often dealers will offer 0 percent financing or a rebate. Which is the better deal? Usually it is better to take the rebate and apply it to the front-end cost of the car and get financing from another source. Let us assume your new car costs $19,287, and you are trading in your old car that is worth $2,000. You can get financing for 4.39 percent. Here is the breakdown of the total costs:

WHICH IS BETTER? COMPARING A $3,000 REBATE AND 0 PERCENT FINANCING

Annual Percentage Rate	0 percent	4.39%
Cost of Car	$19,287	$19,287
Trade-in Value	-$2,000	-$2,000
Rebate	-$0	-$3,000
Amount Financed	$17,287	$14,287
Monthly Payment	$288.12	$265.64
Total Cost	$17,287.20	$15,938.40

By taking the rebate instead of the 0 percent financing, you not only have a lower monthly payment, but the total cost of your loan is over $1,300 less. In fact, the interest rate would have to be as high as 7.7 percent for the rebate *not* to be the better deal. This example assumes you could get the 0 percent financing for 60 months. As discussed above, more often these low rates only apply if the term of the loan is shorter, for example, 36 months. If that is the case, the $17,287 that is financed would be divided by 36 instead of 60, meaning that your monthly payments would be $480.19.

10. No matter where you get your car loan, make sure that there are no penalties for sending in extra payments or prepaying the loan early. Even though it may seem that you will never be in a position to pay off your car early, four to five years is a long time and you never know what will happen. Even if you plan to pay on your car for the full length of the loan, you can use the ability to prepay to get additional money taken off the price of your car. Sometimes dealers will offer you a rebate on a car, but only if you finance through them. If you can find a lower interest rate somewhere else, go ahead and finance through the dealership—making sure you can pay off the loan early with no penalty. The rebate will be applied to the cost of your car, making the amount you finance lower. Get the lower rate financing elsewhere, and use that loan to completely pay off the loan you got from the dealership. This way, you get both a lower price on the car (through the rebate) and a lower interest rate (that you found somewhere else).

Mortgages

Buying your own home is probably the biggest investment (and the largest loan) you will have in your lifetime. A mortgage is simply the name given to the loan you take out to buy a house. A mortgage is an example of a secured loan since if you do not pay on the mortgage the lender can foreclose on the property and seize it. As such, you need to be aware of what the most common types of mortgages are so you can be better prepared to ask the appropriate questions.

As with car loans, the first step in getting a mortgage is to get your credit score and report. If your credit score needs some improvement, you should put off buying a house until you qualify for a lower interest rate. For a loan that is as long as a mortgage typically is, a small difference in interest rate can have a large effect on the total cost of the loan. The table below shows how just a 1 percent difference in the interest rate can affect the monthly payment and the total interest paid.

Interest Rate	5.5%	6.0%	6.5%
Amount Financed	$250,000	$250,000	$250,000
Length of Loan	30 years	30 years	30 years
Monthly Payment	$1,784.06	$1,863.46	$1,944.75
Total Interest Paid Over Life of Loan	$276,322.60	$304,595	$333,548.72

Having a good credit score and getting the lowest possible APR means that your monthly payments will be lower and you will pay much less (over $57,000 in this case) over the life of the loan.

In addition to getting your credit score before you begin the home-buying process, you should also get some quotes on interest rates before you start looking. As with the car buying process, you can get a better idea of what kind of interest rate you can qualify for if you conduct a little research online before you start looking.

Finally, once you have an idea of what kind of interest rate you would qualify for, sit down and work out your budget. Remember in the section on auto loans, it was recommended that you *not* tell the dealer how much of a monthly payment you could afford. Similarly, do not let a mortgage broker tell you how much of a mortgage payment you can afford. Many people get steered into a more expensive mortgage than they can afford because they have turned that decision over to a mortgage broker. You should have a clear idea of what monthly payment you can handle before you begin the process.

While mortgage lenders look at credit scores, they also look at another indicator of your financial health: the *debt-to-income ratio*. Your credit score tells a lender what your payment *history* has been; your debt-to-income ratio tells a lender what your current situation is. The debt-to-income ratio is simply the fraction of your gross income (before taxes) that you pay toward outstanding debt. Mortgage lenders apply what is known as the *28/36 rule* to see how much of a mortgage you qualify for. The first number, 28, is the maximum percentage of your gross income that should go toward housing costs. Be aware that housing costs include more than just the mortgage payment. Included in housing costs are insurance, property taxes, and any other recurring expenses associated with housing (like home owner association dues). The second number, 36, is the maximum percentage of your gross income that should be paid toward housing expenses (covered in the "28" portion), plus other recurring debt. This other debt includes things like car payments, credit card payments (if you are carrying a balance)—any payments that are long-term and recurring.

For example, assume that you are earning $5,000 per month. Your only debt obligation is a car loan with a $250 a month payment. Applying the 28 rule, you can carry housing expense of $1,400 per month ($5,000 × .28), which includes interest, principle, insurance, and taxes. Applying the 36 rule, you can handle a total of $1,800 of debt each month ($5,000 × .36), but $1,400 of that is housing expense. That leaves you with $400 a month for other debt. Your only other debt is your car loan, which is $250, so you would be approved. Be aware, however, of how tight these numbers are. If your car loan were $350 per month, and you were making credit card payments of $150 per month, you would be over the 36 percent maximum. Your only options are to pay off the credit card in full, or to downsize the size of house you look for. If your other recurring debt adds up to $500 per month, you will only have $1,300 to put toward housing expenses.

Fixed versus Adjustable Rate Mortgages

The most basic difference in mortgages is between fixed rate and adjustable rate mortgages. There are other types, which we will discuss, but these are the two main categories.

Fixed rate mortgages are those whose interest rate stays the same over the life of the loan. Whatever interest rate you agree to at the time you sign the mortgage contract is the same rate you will have when you make your last payment. The good news with fixed rate mortgages is that you have certainty when planning your budget in the coming years because your mortgage payment will stay the same. (Note: often property taxes and/or homeowners insurance are also included in the mortgage payments, so monthly payments could change slightly as a result of changes in these amounts over the years). What is good news for you, however, is not good news for the lender. When a lender issues you a mortgage at a fixed rate for 20 to 30 years, that lender is taking on substantial risk because the economy can change drastically over that period of time. An interest rate that is profitable for the lender today may not be in another decade due to changes in economic conditions. Because the lender is taking on risk with fixed rate mortgages, the interest rates tend to be higher than those for adjustable rate mortgages.

Adjustable rate mortgages (ARMs) are usually not completely adjustable. They usually start off as fixed rate mortgages for a period of three to seven years. After this initial period, however, the interest rate can change since it is tied to an index, such as securities issued by the Treasury. If the index falls, your monthly payments will also fall; however, if the index rises, your monthly payment will as well. While interest rates on ARMs typically do not change every month, they do follow a fixed "adjustment" schedule. For example, a 5/1 ARM is an adjustable rate mortgage that is fixed for the first five years, with the interest rate subject to change every year thereafter. ARMs usually are issued with caps in place to offer some consumer protection. Caps are limits on how high the interest rate can increase. Interest rates for ARMs are usually initially lower than those for fixed rate mortgages since the lender is protected from risk by the ability to increase interest rates.

So which is better, a fixed or adjustable mortgage? It depends. If you think you will be in your house for many years, a fixed rate is probably the best option. On

A young couple buys a new house. According to the Bureau of Labor Statistics, 10 percent of those under 25 years of age were homeowners with a mortgage in 2009. (*Shutterstock*)

the other hand, if you plan on selling the house once the initial period is over on an adjustable mortgage, you can benefit from the lower interest rates during the first years and then sell the house when the adjustment kicks in. Alternatively, you can *refinance* your house when the initial period is over. When you refinance your house, you simply replace your existing mortgage with a new one, presumably one with a lower interest rate. Both of these strategies, however, depend upon your house appreciating in value while you own it.

For example, assume you bought a house with a 5/1 ARM in 2003, financing $300,000. Your interest rate was fixed for five years, and in 2009, became adjustable. Assume that the "adjusted" interest rate is so high that you want to refinance your mortgage. But you discover that in 2009, your house is only valued at $220,000. You will not be able to refinance your house because you owe more on the house than it is worth. If you sell it, you will still owe the lender the difference between the amount you borrowed and what you can get for you house in the current market. As the financial meltdown of 2008–09 taught us, houses do not always increase in value.

Balloon loans are a hybrid of fixed and adjustable rate mortgages, at least in the beginning. For a certain amount of time (usually seven to 10 years), the loan has a fixed rate of interest, but the rate is usually lower than that of standard fixed rate loans. The rates are closer to those of adjustable rate mortgages in the beginning period. However, after the initial period, the entire remaining balance of the loan is due. People who take out balloon loans do not expect to have the money to pay these loans off, of course. They plan on refinancing the mortgage before the balloon payment is due. But, again, at the time of refinancing, there are two things that are uncertain, the value of your house and what the current interest rate will be.

Interest-only loans are mortgages where in the early period of the loan your monthly payment is only going toward paying interest—the principle is not being paid down. After the initial period, your monthly payment will increase, sometimes significantly. As with balloon loans, consumers who take out interest-only loans are counting on the value of their homes to increase so they can sell or refinance after the initial period.

Regardless of the type of mortgage, part of the cost of buying a house includes *points*. Points are simply fees assessed by the lender for making the loan, and are expressed as a percentage. For example, a loan with three points attached means that the lender is charging 3 percent of the loan amount for making the loan. The amount of points that a lender charges can vary, but should be in the neighborhood of three to four points.

Home equity loans are loans that consumers can get once they have built up some equity in their homes. Equity is the difference between what the market value of an asset is and what is still owed on it. For example, if you own a house that is currently worth $200,000 and you still owe $125,000 on it, you have $75,000 worth of equity in your home. Home equity loans (also called second mortgages) are secured loans because in the case of default, the lender can take the property.

Consumers use home equity loans for a variety of reasons, ranging from paying off other, more expensive debt, to financing home improvements, to paying for college. With some types of home equity loans, the consumer borrows the full amount of the loan, up to the credit limit. These loans have a fixed interest rate and a fixed payment period. Home equity lines of credit, on the other hand, allow consumers to borrow whatever amount is needed up to the credit limit. Once established, a line of credit is accessed by simply writing a check against the approved balance. Repayment is based on a variable interest rate, tied to an index.

Since home equity loans typically have a lower interest rate than credit card balances or car loans, some consumers use the equity in their homes to consolidate their credit card debt and/or to purchase a car. While the lower interest rate may be attractive, remember than any time a loan is taken out against the equity in your home, if you fail to make payments your home can be taken from you.

Home equity loans should only be used if you are certain that they can be repaid on time.

Student Loans

Paying college tuition with borrowed money has become increasingly common over the past 20 years or so and potentially represents a good use of credit. Borrowing money to buy something that will (hopefully) increase in value is an investment, unlike borrowing money to buy a new iPod. The recent changes in the laws governing student loans make it much easier to borrow and offer some forgiveness in repayment.

Beginning in 2010, students who want a federal student loan to attend college will apply through only one source, the Direct Loan program. All colleges and universities will participate in this program, so once an application is made, the school determines the amount of the loan and sends you the contract. Because this is a federal student loan program, the interest rates are lower than they would be for privately obtained loans. The contract stipulates your responsibilities for repayment. If you take out a loan after July 1, 2014, you may petition to have your loan payments capped at 10 percent of your income, down from the previous cap of 15 percent. In addition, after you have paid on your student loan for 20 years, the balance of the loan will be forgiven.

LOAN CONTRACTS

Whether you are borrowing money to buy a car, a house, or a refrigerator, every loan will require you to sign a contract. Contracts can be very complex, so it is important that you ask about portions you do not understand. Remember that contracts are written to protect the lender, not you. While the specifics of each contract will vary, there are four components that you should be particularly aware of:

1. Acceleration clause. If an *acceleration clause* is included, it means that if you miss just one payment, the lender is entitled to collect the entire balance of the loan. Sometimes the lender will not act on this clause if you make a good faith effort to make your payments, but you certainly cannot count on it.

2. Recourse clause. A *recourse clause* states that if you are not making payments, then the lender has the right to collect the balance of the loan through *garnishing* your wages (a legal action wherein your employer is required to send your wages directly to whomever has placed the garnishment). If you have put up any assets as collateral, the recourse clause also permits the lender to seize that property to satisfy the outstanding balance of the loan.

3. Deficiency clause. The recourse clause (#2, above) says that the lender can seize any collateral to satisfy the loan. The *deficiency clause* says that if, after the lender sells the seized collateral, you still have an outstanding balance, you still owe that amount. For example, let us assume that you owe $3,000 on a loan, and you cannot pay it. Under the recourse clause, if you have put your car up as collateral on the loan, the lender can seize your car and sell it. If the lender only gets $2,000 for your car, you still owe the lender $1,000 under the deficiency clause. You must

also pay for the costs the lender incurred in selling your assets.

4. Insurance clause. Sometimes the lender requires you to purchase insurance that will pay off the loan in the event of your death. The *insurance clause* is most often used with mortgages.

BORROWING ONLINE

The explosion of online lenders represents good news for consumers because it increases competition, resulting in lower interest rates. Both online and on-the-ground lenders will require the same information from you before they approve a loan, but online lenders can offer some advantages. As discussed in the previous sections on car and home loans, it is always a good idea to know the size of loan you qualify for before talking to a dealer or mortgage broker. Therefore, even if you do not end up getting your loan from an online lender, applying for online loans is a way for you to get more information going into the purchase. Many online lenders offer interest rate and loan quotes for free, and they do it very quickly, so the cost to you of getting this information is minimal. In addition, online lenders typically offer 24 hour customer service. Dealing with online businesses can be risky, however, so you need to be sure that you are dealing with a reputable company. A good indicator that you should *not* do business with an online lender is if they ask for a payment before you qualify for a loan. Whether it is called a referral fee, a processing fee or a prequalification fee, you should never pay it.

SUMMARY

Consumers need to borrow money for a variety of reasons and having access to credit certainly makes life easier, whether you need to buy a car, a house, or pay for college tuition. A good first place to start any loan process is your credit report and credit score. Without this information you may find yourself paying too much for any kind of loan. We look more closely at these two pieces of information in the next chapter.

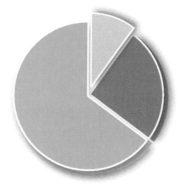

Credit Reports
and Scores

One number can hold the key to your financial success. One number can determine if you get a car or a house and how much you will pay for it. One number can even determine if you get a job. Do you know what yours is and how it compares to the average? Most Americans do not. What is this all-powerful number? It is your credit score. The bad news about a credit score is that it is used in a variety of ways, from loan approvals to employment, so if yours is bad, your financial life will suffer. The good news is that credit scores can be improved.

Before we talk about how to improve your credit score, you need to understand what it is, where it comes from, and how your behavior affects it. The first thing to know is that a credit report and a credit score, while related, are not the same thing. Since your credit score is based upon your credit report, we will start by looking at credit reporting.

CREDIT REPORTS

Every time you fill out a credit application, every time you make a payment (or do not), every time you cancel a credit card or just change your address, your actions are being monitored by one or more of the country's three credit reporting agencies: *Experian, Equifax,* and *TransUnion.* You (indirectly) provide information to these agencies when you fill out credit applications, but the bulk of the information provided about you comes from the companies you do business with. Your bill payment history, including late payments, any bankruptcies, court-ordered payments (like child support or alimony)—all of it is included in your credit history. Every month, lenders and financial institutions send information about all of their customers to one, two, or all three of the credit reporting agencies. These agencies compile all of this information into reports that summarize your financial life, and then make them available to lenders and financial institutions to use in deciding whether to extend your credit or not and at what interest rate.

Credit reporting agencies are not new. In fact, they have been around for decades. It was not until 1971, however, that Congress passed the Fair Credit Reporting Act (FCRA) to set standards about what information the agencies could gather and in what form. In an updated version of the FCRA passed in 2001, consumers have direct access to both their reports and scores. In a further update in 2004, consumers are entitled to one free copy of their credit report each year from each of the three credit reporting agencies. With this increased access comes

GETTING YOUR CREDIT REPORTS

You can access all three reports by

1. Visiting www.annualcreditreport.com
   or
2. Phoning 877-322-8228

increased responsibility to check your reports, verify their accuracy, and report incorrect information.

You should get your credit reports from all three credit reporting agencies every year. The reports will not be identical, and information that appears on one may not appear on the others. You should also time your credit report request to put you in the best position when applying for a loan. For example, if you are applying for a car loan or mortgage, you should request your credit reports about six months before you want to apply for the loan. This will give you time to check the report, correct any errors, or improve some items if need be. Be aware that there are many companies that claim to provide you with credit reports. These are scams. You should only get your reports directly from one of the credit reporting agencies or from the Web site in the box above. See chapter 6 for more information about avoiding scams.

Reading Your Reports

The three reporting agencies present information in different ways, but they all have four basic parts. The first part contains identifying information, such as your name, social security number, your present and previous addresses, and date of birth. The second part contains your credit history. The reports are generally written in very easy-to-understand language: "never late with a payment," or "default on loan." Each account that you have had appears here with its detail, including

- whether it is your account or if someone else is on the account with you
- what kind of account it is (for example, a car loan)
- the total amount of the loan (or, if it is a credit card, the credit limit)
- the balance of the loan
- the monthly payments (or, minimum payments, if a credit card)
- the status of your account (that is, whether it is paid, open, etc.)
- your payment history on the account (whether you have paid on time, how many times you have paid late)

Another section of a credit report is the public section. This is the section that will list any financial activity that is a matter of public record, such as bankruptcies, garnishments, nonpayment of taxes. It is good when this section is empty.

Finally, the report contains a list of everyone who has asked to see your credit report. If you apply for a loan, the potential lender will ask for your credit report and generate an inquiry. When you ask for a copy of your report, it will generate an inquiry. Both of these are examples of "hard" inquiries. "Soft" inquiries are generated when companies request lists of consumers for the purpose of sending out credit card offers, for example.

If you find an error on your report, you need to correct it immediately. A possible error could be that your credit report shows a loan balance or monthly payment amount that is different from what it actually is. The credit report could also list a purchase for which you did not accept delivery. The report could even list activity that you did not engage in—perhaps someone who was not authorized to access your account made some purchases. Whatever the error, you will need to send a letter to each reporting agency that is reporting the error. In the letter, you should provide detailed information about the error, including a copy of the credit report with the error highlighted. Upon receipt of your letter, the credit reporting agency will conduct its own investigation, contacting the creditor from whom they got the information. Until the dispute is resolved, the credit reporting agency may not send out information to other creditors that might damage your credit score.

If the creditor admits that it made a mistake, the credit reporting agency will correct the information on your report. If the creditor does not admit an error and/or the matter is not resolved to your satisfaction, you have the right to write a statement explaining your side of the dispute and place it in your report. This statement will then be included in all future reports that are sent out.

CREDIT SCORES

As important as credit scores are to consumers' financial well-being, almost half of Americans do not know what their credit score is. Actually, you have more than one credit score, but the one most commonly used is a FICO score (Fair Isaac Corporation). Each credit reporting agency, using the information it has collected on you,

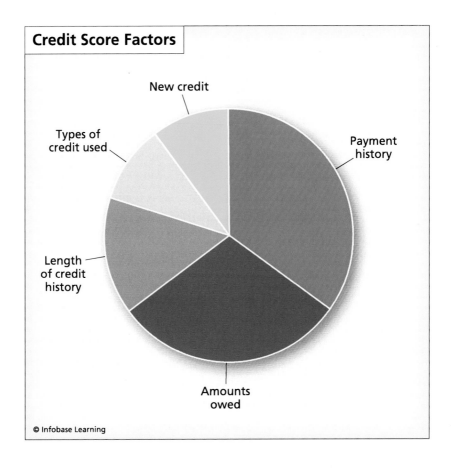

Credit Score Factors

New credit

Types of
credit used

Payment
history

Length
of credit
history

Amounts
owed

© Infobase Learning

generates its own score, so it is likely that you have three different scores. While you are entitled to one free credit report from each agency once a year, you cannot get your credit score for free unless you have been denied a credit card. You must pay for your FICO score by going to www. myfico.com. You can also get credit scores from each of the three credit reporting agencies from www.annualcreditreport.com. These scores are not FICO scores, but can give you an idea of what your FICO score is.

A variety of factors goes into the computation of your score, following the items that are contained in your credit report. The weight of each component is as follows:

- Payment History (35 percent). Your payment history—whether you pay on time—is the largest piece of your credit score. Payments to credit card companies, cell phone companies, utility companies, mortgages, car loans—all are included. The most recent payment record is weighted more heavily than behavior in the distant past.

- Amounts Owed (30 percent). This category includes how much money you still owe on your accounts, as you might suspect, but also how many accounts you have, and what your credit limits on those accounts are. It is not uncommon for people with very high credit limits to use that credit, making them riskier. Your number will be lower if you carry balances that are close to your limits.

- Length of Credit History (15 percent). The longer your credit history, the more information the reporting agencies have on you, and therefore, the better able they are to accurately assess your credit risk.

- Types of Credit (10 percent). Similar to the length of credit history, the more types of credit you have (car loan, credit cards), the easier it is for the agencies to get accurate information on your credit risk. In particular, your credit score will be higher if you have a mix of revolving credit (for example, credit cards) and installment loans (car loans, or mortgages).

- New Credit (10 percent). This component reflects how many times you have applied for credit recently. If you are applying for new credit because you have been late with payments to existing credit cards, for example, your credit score will take a hit. If you are applying for new credit because you are trying to find the best deal in an auto loan or mortgage, you will not be penalized.

When you get your score, you will also get detailed information on how you rate on each component (very good, good, etc.). You will also be given information on what is hurting your score and how you can improve it.

What Is a Good Score?

Credit scores range from 300 to 850, with higher scores representing better financial situations. As of 2009, the national average FICO score was about 700, which is generally considered a good score. Following is the distribution of FICO scores in the United States:

NATIONAL CREDIT SCORES	PERCENTAGE OF POPULATION
300–499	2%
500–549	5%
550–599	8%
600–649	12%
650–699	15%
700–749	18%
750–799	27%
800–850	13%

The score that is considered low enough to qualify as "subprime" (that is, risky), changes with economic conditions. As a result of the 2008–09 financial meltdown, consumers who had previously been considered creditworthy, found themselves unable to get credit, or only able to get it by paying very high interest rates. Typically, a score of 600 or less is considered a "bad" score.

If you doubt how important your credit score is, take a look at the following table:

15 YEAR MORTGAGE ($300,000)			48 MONTH CAR LOAN ($25,000)		
Credit Score	Interest Rate	Monthly Payment	Credit Score	Interest Rate	Monthly Payment
760–850	4.096%	$2,234	720–850	5.2%	$578
700–759	4.318%	$2,267	690–719	6.704%	$595
680–699	4.495%	$2,294	660–689	8.281%	$614
660–679	4.708%	$2,327	620–659	11.203%	$649
640–659	5.138%	$2,394	590–619	16.495%	$715
620–639	5.683%	$2,480	500–589	19.234%	$751

If you have a credit score of 620, notice what your situation is when you try to get credit. For a 48-month car loan, financing $25,000, you will pay 11.2 percent on your loan, paying $71 more a month than someone with a credit score of 760. That amounts to another $3,408 over the life of the loan. If you try to get a mortgage, you will pay an extra $246 a month, compared to someone who has a credit score of 760. That's almost $3,000 extra per year. You should also notice that with a credit score of 620, you barely qualify for a mortgage at all.

You may think that lenders are too dependent on credit scores. In fact, lenders know that there is a direct relationship between credit scores and the probability of becoming 90 days delinquent on a mortgage. For example, if your credit score is 600, the odds of delinquency are four to one. However, if your credit score is 780, those odds increase to 576 to one.

Good credit scores are not only necessary for the best deals in interest rates. Many employers are using an applicant's credit score as an additional screening tool in the hiring process. Many employment applications ask you to give the potential employer permission to access your credit score and/or credit report. The assumption is that if your credit score is bad, it is an indicator that you are not responsible and therefore, a less-than-desirable employee. In addition, your credit score may be used by landlords, utility companies, cell phone providers, and others to assess your credit worthiness or responsibility.

How to Improve Your Credit Score

You are convinced of the importance of a high credit score. Unfortunately, you have looked at yours and it is pretty low—too low to get a good interest rate. You have checked out your credit report to make sure there are no errors that could be contributing to your low score, and your report is accurate. What now? Can you improve your credit score?

The simple answer is, yes. But, there are right ways and wrong ways to do so. The wrong way is to pay money to a credit repair service that promises to restore your credit and improve your score. These businesses offer quick fixes to credit problems, but quick fixes do not exist. Increasing your credit score takes time. Save your money and take care of this yourself.

Take a look back at the section that described what
the components of a credit score are. The way to improve
your credit score is to address each of these components.
Let us take them one at a time:

- *Payment History.* Since this is the largest
  component of your credit score, the way to
  improve this aspect is to pay your bills on
  time. You do not need to wait until you need
  credit to do this. If you have little to no credit
  history, borrow money and pay it back—before you need that car loan. Establishing a
  history of repayment is the best thing you
  can do to improve your score. If you have
  already missed a payment or two, get current with that account and stay current. If a
  creditor has turned a past due account over
  to a collections agency, there will be two
  entries on your credit report. The original
  company will "charge off" your debt after six
  months of nonpayment. This does not mean
  that you no longer owe them money—you
  still do. A charge off is just an accounting
  term for a bad debt. After six months, the
  creditor may turn your account over to a
  collections agency to try to get repayment.
  There are now two entries in your credit report: one from the original creditor reporting the charge off, and the second from the
  collections agency. Once your account goes
  to collections, that notation will stay on your
  credit report for seven years, even if you pay
  it off. Finally, if you settle a debt for less than
  what you owe (a work out arrangement with

your credit card company, for example), ask the creditor to report the debt as being "paid in full" rather than "settled." Debts that are settled typically reduce your credit score.

- *Amounts Owed.* As discussed above, this component is not simply the amount of money you owe creditors. It is the ratio of the amount you owe to the amount of credit you have available to you. This is where things can get a little tricky. Let us assume you have three credit cards, each with a credit limit of $1,500. That means your total available credit is $4,500 ($1,500 × 3). This component of your score depends on how much of that $4,500 you actually owe. Obviously, one way to make this a strong category for you is to keep your balances low. If you owe $400 on Card 1, $500 on Card 2 and $600 on Card 3, ($1,500 total), you have used 33 percent of your credit limit ($1,500/$4,500). Let us assume that you pay off Card 1 completely and decide to close that account. That's a good move on your part, right? Maybe not. If you pay off Card 1, your total debt decreases to $1,100 ($500 + $600)—that's a good thing. But, closing the account means that your total available credit also decreases—to $3,000—because you only have two cards left open. This means that your debt ratio has gone up to 37 percent ($1,100/$3,000)—not a good thing. If you had paid off Card 1, as before, but *not* closed out the account, your debt ratio would decrease to 24 percent ($1,100/$4,500). The lesson here is, paying off debt is a good thing, but closing accounts may or may not be. Notice that if you had paid off Card 3 and closed that account, your outstanding debt would be $900, your debt limit would be $3,000, making your debt ratio fall to 30 percent. Before you close any accounts, do some calculations to make sure that you will not be increasing your debt-to-limit ratio. Remember that even when you close an account, the history still appears on your credit report.

You may be thinking that if closing accounts can lower your score, opening accounts can raise your score. Not so fast. While the logic appears to be sound, the reality is that having a low debt-to-limit ratio that is supported by many credit cards will raise your score. There is a limit to how many open accounts the reporting agencies view as favorable. More than three open credit card accounts may begin to lower your score, even if you owe very little on them. Reporting agencies do not like to see high credit limits spread out over many cards—people tend to use the credit they have available to them. In addition, applying for a lot of credit all at one time sends a signal that you are scrambling to try to repair your credit.

- *Length of Credit History.* If you do decide to close some accounts, do not close your oldest accounts—close your most recent accounts first. Credit reporting agencies view favorably a record of good payment history. If you cancel your oldest accounts, that information will still appear on your credit record (remember, when you close an account, it does not erase it from your credit report), but the clock stops ticking on that account. Credit reporting agencies like clocks that have ticked for a long time. This shows them that you are trustworthy and a good credit risk over the long haul.

- *Types of Credit.* Just as with investing, diversify—do not put all your eggs into one basket. The best credit scores reflect a variety of credit: credit cards, cell phone contracts, rental leases, car loans, student loans—all are examples of the types of credit that will improve your score. That being said, opening new types of credit just for the sake of creating a mix is not a good idea. This category is only 10 percent of your score. It is better to take a slight hit in this category than to apply for a lot of different kinds of credit (and risk getting into debt trouble) if you do not really need it.

- *New Credit.* As discussed above, applying for a lot of new credit cards at one time will drive your credit score down. On the other hand, if you are rate shopping for a car loan, for example, make sure you do the comparison shopping within a 30-day period. The FICO calculation distinguishes between the two, and while the former will hurt your score, the latter will not.

The two most important things to remember about increasing your credit score are, first, that it takes time. There are no overnight repairs, in spite of what some credit repair businesses claim. The second thing to remember is that your goal is to paint a picture of yourself as someone who has good lines of credit available to you, but that you use them in moderation.

SUMMARY

Your ability to get credit, how much that credit will cost, your ability to get a job, to get an apartment, a cell phone—all depend, in large part, on your credit report and your credit score. In this chapter, you learned what these two pieces of information are, what their components are, and how you can influence them. Your ability to maintain a good report and score allows you to participate in the economy in the mainstream credit market. A poor report and a low score mean that you will be unable to get credit at all or you will only have access to it through the secondary credit market where rates are high and options are limited. The next chapter addresses the options that exist in the alternative market.

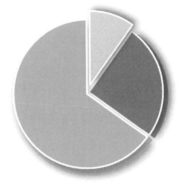

5

Alternative Loans

As we have seen, access to credit from mainstream lenders is determined, to a large extent, by your credit score. If you have a good credit score, you will not only have access to credit from mainstream lenders, but it will be at a low relative cost. But what if your credit history is not particularly good and your score is low? How do you get credit when the mainstream institutions turn you down?

There are alternatives to mainstream lending institutions, and this chapter outlines several of these options. Be aware that with all of them, the costs are significant.

PAYDAY LOANS

You have probably seen the signs for payday loan businesses in your community. Established in the 1990s, the payday lending industry has over 22,000 locations across the country. *Payday loans* are marketed as a way for consumers to get small, emergency loans (for example, for car repairs)—the kind of unsecured loan that a bank or credit union typically would not grant based on the small amount of the loan and/or the consumer's credit history.

Here is how a payday loan works. Let us say you need $300 to fix the transmission on your car. Your credit cards are maxed out (or you do not have any), you have no emergency savings fund—you have no way to get the money to pay for your car repairs. To make matters worse, you will not get paid for another two weeks, and you need your car now. So you go to a payday lender. The payday lender will accept a postdated check from you, or a signed authorization to withdraw funds from your checking account. A postdated check is a check with a date that is sometime in the future. The person you write the check to cannot cash the check until the date that is on the check, so if you postdate the check for 14 days into the future, the payday lender cannot cash the check until that future date. On that date, you will get your paycheck and plan to have funds in your account to cover the check that the payday lender will then cash. So, you give the payday lender a postdated check, and you get your loan, minus a lender's "fee" of about $50. You walk away with $250, and the payday lender holds your check until your next payday, or when your check was postdated. On that day, the loan is due in full—$300. You might recognize that this is an example of a balloon loan (from chapter 3), where the entire amount is due on a specified day.

Three things can happen at this point. The first is that you pay back the entire amount of the loan and your need for a payday loan is over. Your car is fixed, you can meet the rest of your monthly bills with the money you have left after you have paid back the loan. The second thing that can happen is that for some reason, when the

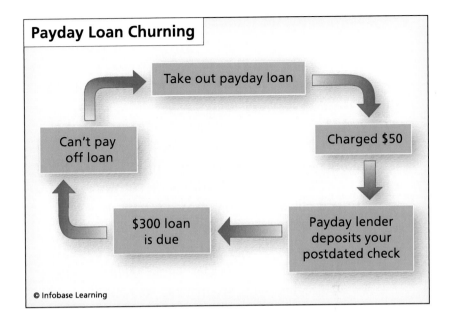

Payday Loan Churning

Take out payday loan

Charged $50

Payday lender deposits your postdated check

$300 loan is due

Can't pay off loan

© Infobase Learning

payday lender deposits your check for payment, you do not have sufficient funds in your account to cover it. The bank will charge you a bounced check fee for every time the payday lender tries to collect payment, and the lender can try to deposit your check repeatedly. The third possible outcome is the most common. You discover that paying back the $300 means you cannot meet all your monthly obligations. You can either pay another $50 to keep the loan outstanding (you are simply extending the time when you must pay back the original $300), or you pay back the $300 and then immediately take out another loan to cover your shortfall. In either case, you have paid another $50. If the same thing happens during your next pay period, you will find yourself paying another $50 to avoid default on the original loan. This is called "churning" your loan. Every two weeks you will pay $50 just to keep your original loan afloat, while never paying down the original amount.

Unfortunately, the third alternative is where many consumers who utilize payday loans find themselves. Of the consumers who use a payday lender, over 80 percent take out more than one loan in a year's time. Half of these borrowers' loans occur in the very next pay period after paying back the original loan. In other words, the period between paying off an existing loan and taking out another one is a day or less. Over three-quarters of payday loans are churned in a time period of two weeks or less. The resulting "fees" mean that the effective APR on these types of loans are routinely around 400 percent. Researchers have found that the typical consumer utilizing a payday lender will pay $500 for a $300 loan—and still not have paid back the original loan amount.

Clearly, payday loans should be approached with extreme caution. Consumers who use payday lenders for the first time never dream they will be caught in this debt trap. However, only 2 percent of payday loans are made to consumers who take out only one loan—nonrepeat customers. Because the profits from the payday loan industry come from churning loans, sometimes payday lenders will offer first-time borrowers very low (or free) loans in order to attract new customers. In addition, those who utilize payday lenders double their odds of finding themselves in bankruptcy, compared to those who have been denied a payday loan. Over one-half of those who borrow from payday lenders will find themselves in default in the first year of the loan.

CAR TITLE LOANS

Like payday loans, *car title loans* are offered to consumers as small loans to help in an emergency situation. However, as with payday loans, consumers can easily find themselves in a debt trap. Unlike payday loans, however, car title loans use your car as collateral to secure the debt. This means that if you fail to pay back the loan, the title company has the right to take your car. Here is how it works.

You need cash for some sort of emergency—let us assume you have to get some dental work done, and you do not have the money in a savings account to cover the cost. You have seen the advertisements on television about car title loans, and it seems this is the answer to your problem. Car title loans are made for a short period of time—usually 30 days or less. The interest rate that you will probably be quoted will be an interest rate for that amount of time. For example, if you are told that the interest rate on your loan will be 25 percent, you may think that is not so bad. After all, your credit card has an APR of 18 percent, so 25 percent for an emergency loan like this is not horrible, right? Wrong! Your credit card's interest rate is expressed as an APR—annual percentage rate. In other words, over the course of an entire year, the interest rate would be 18 percent. Notice that the 25 percent quoted on the car title loan is not expressed as an APR—it is the interest rate for one month and one month only. If the interest rate is 25 percent for one month, the APR would be approximately 300 percent (25 percent × 12)! This does not sound like such a good deal anymore, does it? If you take out an $800 loan, that means that at the end of the month you will owe the original $800, plus interest, for a total of $1,000.

Again, three things can happen. The first is that you pay the $1,000 at the end of 30 days, and everything is fine. The second is that you cannot pay the $1,000 at the end of the month, and the car title loan company takes your car. The third possibility is that they do not take your car, but they give you the opportunity to "refinance" your loan. At the end of the month, instead of paying the total amount of what you owe—$1,000—you pay back the interest, $200. This puts you right back where you started from, owing $800, and starts the clock over again on the accumulating interest. And the end of the second month, you will owe $1,000 again, and so it goes. By law, a car title loan cannot be rolled over more than six times. If you roll your loan over that many times, you will have paid $1,200 in interest on an $800 loan, which you still have not paid back. At the end of the sixth time, your car will be taken. As you can see, it is often in the best interests of the car title lender to not take your car after the first month of nonpayment. More profit is made by rolling this loan over than repossessing the car and disposing of it, particularly if the company is going to end up with your car after six months anyway.

REFUND ANTICIPATION LOANS

Unlike payday loans and car title loans, you only hear about *refund anticipation loans* at one time during the year—tax time. A refund anticipation loan (RAL) is offered by tax preparers, and is a small loan that is secured by the taxpayer's anticipated refund. The loans usually are very short-term—one to two weeks. To get a refund anticipation loan, you go to a tax preparer advertising "instant refunds," give the preparer your income and other information for the past year, and they will prepare and file your tax return for you. At the same time that they submit your tax return to the IRS electronically, they also submit your information to a bank that is participating in making RALs. Once the bank approves your loan application (often in less than a day), you will be issued a check, secured by your refund. The amount of this check is your refund minus any fees charged by the tax preparer and any loan expenses charged by the bank. When you refund arrives from the IRS, it is deposited into the lending bank, repaying your loan. Notice that they are loaning you your own money!

Refund anticipation loans are very costly to consumers. Lower income consumers are particularly vulnerable because of their increased need for funds, and their relative unfamiliarity with tax preparation. To see how costly an RAL is, let us look at the following example (taken from the Web site of Total-tax-service.com). Assume you qualify for a tax refund of $2,500. The tax preparer charges you a $39 processing and documentation fee, the bank charges a $32 processing fee, the tax software company charges a $12.95 technology fee, and the bank charges an additional 1 percent of the loan amount, or $25. These fees add up to $108.95, and you still owe a tax preparation fee. Omitting that fee for the moment, $108.95 charged on a loan of $2,500 is an interest rate of 4.4 percent. That's a great loan rate, isn't it? Wait a minute—remember APR? You are paying 4.4 percent on a loan that is a very short-term loan, usually between one and two weeks. Assuming that the loan is for 10 days, the APR on this loan becomes 157 percent! And, again, you still have not paid the tax preparation fee. The smaller the RAL, the higher the APR when these fees are included because most of the fees are fixed amounts. Paying a $39 processing fee on a loan of $2,500 is a smaller percentage than if the loan amount were only $300. Doing the same calculations for a $300 RAL results in an APR of over 1,000 percent.

Refund anticipation loans are offers to loan you your own money at a very high interest rate. The biggest advantage to RALs was the speed with which you could get your refund, but since the IRS began offering e-filing, that advantage has disappeared. You can file your taxes yourself electronically and get your refund directly deposited into your checking account in about two weeks, with no additional fees. If you are not sure about how to fill out the tax forms, you can get free help by going to a VITA (Volunteer Income Tax Assistance) site (call 1-800-906-9887 or visit the IRS.gov Web site for site locations).

OVERDRAFT PROTECTION

When you open a checking account at a bank or credit union, you will be offered *overdraft protection.* "Protection" does not sound like a loan, does it? But, it is. The way overdraft protection works is if you write a check or use your debit card and spend more than what is in your account, the financial institution will cover your shortfall. If they did not cover it, you would be charged an insufficient funds fee, plus the merchants where you wrote the bad checks would also charge you a returned check fee. So the overdraft protection is to "protect" you from the merchants' returned check fee. Sounds like a good deal. But, this protection comes at a high price. Every time the institution needs to cover your overage, they still charge you the insufficient funds, or overdraft fee, usually about $34. If you have miscalculated how much money is in your account and are out running errands, you are charged $34 every time your balance goes below zero. If you buy a book at the bookstore, then grab some lunch, and then pick up some dry cleaning, you can be charged $34 each of these three times if you are overdrawn. That is $102 more than what you thought you were spending. When the financial institution subtracts these fees, you are further in the hole than you were before. Notice that if you had tried to use your debit card (instead of writing checks) in these three instances and did *not* have overdraft protection, your card would have simply been denied—you would not have been assessed any fees.

The average amount that an account is overdrawn is about $17. Since the bank or credit union is charging you $34 for what is really a $17 loan (it will be repaid as soon as you make another deposit), overdraft protection is really a short-term loan. You will be assessed the $34 fee regardless of how much overdrawn your account is. Thus, being overdrawn by just $1 will trigger the $34 fee.

In addition, the way that some banks and credit unions handle debits to your account can increase these fees. Assume you have $20 in your account. You use your debit card to buy a book for $15, then later in the day you use it to buy something for $50. You may think that you would be assessed an overdraft fee of $34 only once because you had money in your account to cover the book (your first purchase) and the other charge did not come until later in the day. Unfortunately, financial institutions do not have to post debits to your account in the order in which they occurred. Instead, they can post them from highest to lowest. In this case, you would be assessed the $34 fee twice because the largest debit amount of $50 put you immediately in the red, followed by the $15 book purchase. Recent changes in the law require that banks not automatically enroll you in overdraft protection plans—you must be given the choice to opt in. As an alternative, you can link your checking account to your savings account, allowing overdraft funds to be transferred into your checking account automatically without fees.

SUMMARY

When your credit is poor, or when you have little or no savings for emergencies, you may be forced to consider alternative loans when you are faced with an expected expense. The best option, of course, is to make sure you have an emergency fund so that you do not have to utilize these businesses. Payday loans and car title loans often trap people in a cycle of indebtedness that they cannot break. The best course of action is: Do not use them. Investigate all your other options (including doing without whatever you need the money for) before you use any of these businesses.

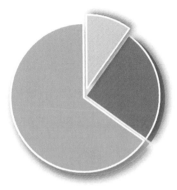

6

Credit Problems

As we have discovered, credit can be a wonderful thing. It allows us to purchase things that we otherwise would not be able to, or would only be able to after years of disciplined saving. Credit, and the resulting debt, can also lead to heartache and sleepless nights. Sometimes, in spite of their best intentions, consumers can find themselves overextended, unable to make payments, taking (or avoiding) calls from collection agencies.

If you find yourself in trouble with your credit (see the 10 warning signs on page 92), there are several ways to address the problem. Whatever means you choose, the most important thing to remember is that ignoring the problem will not make it go away. As difficult as money problems are to face, not facing them will compound the problem. So, let us look at some alternatives that exist for consumers who need help with their debt.

DOING IT ON YOUR OWN

Often consumers can deal with their credit and debt problems themselves if they understand what options are open to them. The first and most important rule if you find yourself in a credit hole is—stop digging! If your credit cards are up to their limits, stop using them. As obvious as this seems, many people continue behaving in the same way that got them into trouble in the first place.

The second step to getting a handle on your debt is to make a budget. Setting a budget was covered in the first volume of this series, but basically, you need to itemize all your expenses. Figure out what expenses are fixed—that stay the same from month to month. These would be things like your rent, car payment, and student loan pay-

10 Warning Signs of Too Much Debt

- You do not know how much debt you have
- You are at or above your credit card limit for one or more cards.
- Your checking account is frequently overdrawn.
- You have been denied credit.
- You are sometimes late with credit card or other loan payments.
- You use cash advances from your credit cards to pay other bills.
- You keep using your credit cards, even while trying to pay them off.
- You do not have any money saved.
- You only make the minimum payments on your cards.
- You lie to others about your spending and debt.

Budgeting Web Sites

- http:///www.clearpointcreditcounselingsolutions.org/ credit_ counseling_monthly.aspx.
- http:///www.youcandealwithit.com/borrowers/calculators -and-resources/calculators/budget-calculator.shtml
- http:///www.ehow.com/how_4901098_create-budget- online.html

ments. Make a list of your variable expenses—expenses that change from month to month. Examples of variable expenses would be food, entertainment, and clothing. See what you can eliminate from both lists. Can you start buying some generic items at the grocery store instead of name brands? Can you reduce your cable service or eliminate it completely? What are you paying for cell phone service—can that be reduced or eliminated? The goal here is to figure out how much you can put toward paying down your debt. You can find books on budgeting in the library, or there are many online tools to help with creating a budget.

The third step is to contact your creditors and explain the situation to them. Tell them that you want to work out a payment plan that you can afford. Sometimes credit card companies will "settle" your debt—accept less than what you actually owe. They would rather get something than nothing, so they may agree to a repayment plan that pays back some, but not all, of your debt. If your credit card company does agree to settle your debt, be sure to ask them to indicate that your debt is paid in full once you have fulfilled your agreement, rather than indicating that it is settled. This appears on your credit report, and your score will be lowered if you have settled debts.

If you cannot work out a repayment plan, start paying off the credit cards with the highest interest rate first. You will be carrying balances from month to month, so the sooner you can get rid of the most expensive debt, the better. When you pay off a credit card, add the payments you were making on that card to the next card on the list, with the next-highest interest rate, and so on.

If you are falling behind on a car loan, you cannot afford to wait until the situation is dire. Unlike credit card debt, a car loan is secured by the car. This means that your car can be repossessed with no advance notice. If your car is repossessed, you will probably not be able to get it back by simply bringing your account current. Usually to get back a repossessed car, you must pay off the balance of the loan, plus the cost of towing. Therefore, it is very important to try to work out an arrangement the moment you recognize that you are headed for trouble.

GETTING HELP

If you decide that your situation is too complicated, or you do not have the discipline to develop a budget and stick to it, you can get help from a *credit counseling agency.* Not all credit counseling agencies are the same, however, and even those who say they are nonprofit may not be reputable.

To make sure you are not taken advantage of, you should find out which credit counseling agencies are members of either the National Foundation for Credit Counseling (nfcc.org) or the Association of Independent Consumer Credit Counseling Agencies (aiccca.org). The members of both of these organizations must meet standards, giving you some reassurance of the quality

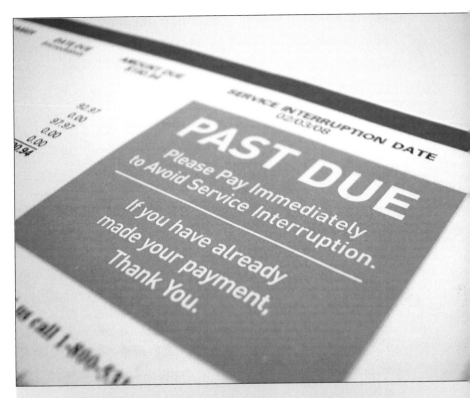

According to the Center for Responsible Lending, people in the 18–24 age bracket spend nearly 30 percent of their monthly income on debt repayment. (*Shutterstock*)

and integrity of the advice you are getting. You can also check with your community's Better Business Bureau to see what agencies have had complaints filed against them.

When you find one or two agencies, you should verify which services they offer at no charge, and what other services they offer and what the fees are. Sometimes agencies will charge an upfront fee and/or a monthly fee for their services. Nonprofit does not mean that all services are free. Credit counseling agencies can help you develop a budget, manage your debt and discuss strategies to get your finances in order. Although you can usually take the same steps on your own that a credit counseling agency would, the discipline of the agency's involvement in an individual's finances can sometimes mean the difference between getting back on track or sinking further in debt.

Sometimes a credit counseling agency will recommend a debt management plan. With a debt management plan, the credit counseling agency works out a repayment plan with your creditors. You deposit money each month with the credit counseling agency, which in turn, uses it to pay your unsecured debt according to the agreement. A debt management plan can last for many years and may require you to not apply for (or perhaps, use) credit while you are covered by the plan.

Under new regulations from the *Federal Trade Commission,* these companies can now only charge a fee once the debt has been reduced or settled. In addition, when payments are required from the consumer, these payments must be made to an independent financial institution.

Many businesses have appeared that promise to "repair" your credit. These businesses are not the same as the credit counseling agencies discussed above. Credit repair companies often claim that they can erase bankruptcies, or restore good credit. Sometimes these companies advise their clients to get a new social security number, creating a new credit history. Or, they will tell their clients to file for a federal employer identification number (which is like a social security number for businesses) and start a new credit report under that number. Both of these strategies are illegal. They may also try to challenge every negative item on the credit report. While this is legal, be aware that creditors are entitled to report negative entries for up to seven years, and up to 10 years if it is bankruptcy.

DEBT CONSOLIDATION

When consumers find themselves mired in a lot of debt, they sometimes turn to debt consolidation loans as a way out. A *debt consolidation loan* is a loan that pays off all or a significant part of many other loans. Smaller loans, such as credit cards and car loans, are combined and replaced by a loan that pays off these other loans. Almost all debt consolidation loans are secured loans, such as home equity loans. The consumer borrows on the equity in their home, then uses that money to pay off the other debts. The major advantage of debt consolidation is that it replaces many monthly payments with a single, lower payment. The disadvantages are that while the debt consolidation loan has a lower monthly payment, the total debt that you owe has not decreased—it is the same. The payment is lower because the term of the loan is longer, meaning you will be paying on the combined loan for a long period of time. The other disadvantage is that because the debt consolidation loan is usually a home equity loan or second mortgage secured by your home, if you find yourself unable to make these payments, you run the risk of losing your home. In addition, if there is no change in behavior, a debt consolidation loan may just delay the inevitable. For example, if you get into trouble with credit card debt and take out a debt consolidation loan, these credit card debts will be paid off and replaced by a loan with lower monthly payments over a longer period of time, secured by your home. If you do not change the behavior that caused the credit card debt in the first place, you may continue to use your credit cards recklessly, running up debt again. This time, however, you do not have the ability to cover that debt with a debt consolidation loan since that equity has already been tapped. Now you have new credit card debt, plus the debt consolidation loan, putting you at significant risk for bankruptcy or foreclosure.

BANKRUPTCY

Unfortunately, sometimes consumers get so far into debt that the only solution is to declare bankruptcy. *Bankruptcy* is a legal arrangement whereby all or many of your debts are erased. What many people do not know is that there are actually two forms of personal bankruptcy, *Chapter 7* and *Chapter 13* ("chapter" refers to the section of the bankruptcy laws).

Chapter 7 (liquidation) is what most people think of when they think of when they think of bankruptcy. With Chapter 7, most of your debts are discharged—they are written off and you no longer have to pay them. In return, a *trustee* (a person appointed by the court to oversee your case) will sell some of your assets to pay your creditors. Your credit report will include the bankruptcy for 10 years.

Although your debts are discharged under Chapter 7, you may decide that you do not want to discharge all of your debts. Why would anyone choose to keep part of their debt if having too much debt is the problem? If you choose to discharge secured debt, like a car loan, it usually requires you to give up the collateral—that means you will lose the car. So, keeping the car loan (and the car) may be a better option than giving it up.

If the court determines that you should be able to repay a significant portion of your debt, you will not be allowed to declare Chapter 7. Under Chapter 13 (wage earner) bankruptcy you repay your debts under a court-approved plan, again under the supervision of a trustee. You do not need to relinquish your assets. Chapter 13 bankruptcy is usually pursued by consumers who believe that their financial troubles are temporary. Chapter 13 bankruptcies can also remain on credit reports for 10 years, although it could be for a shorter length of time (depending on the state) if the debt is paid off before then.

CONSUMER RIGHTS

Although credit issues can seem overwhelming, you have many rights as a consumer in obtaining and maintaining credit, or if you find yourself in trouble. Your rights are enforced by a government agency, the Federal Trade Commission (FTC). The following are just some of the rights you have. To see a complete list, go to the FTC.gov Web site.

- You are entitled to a free copy of your credit report from each of the three credit reporting agencies once per year.
- You are entitled to a free copy of your credit report if you have been denied credit, an apartment, employment, or service based on your report. You must be given the name of the reporting agency that supplied the information. You have 60 days to request a copy of the report.
- You are entitled to know who has accessed your report within the past year.
- You are entitled to dispute any entry on your credit report. Once you have filed a dispute, the credit reporting agency and the entity that provided the disputed information are required to investigate and notify you of the outcome. If you disagree with the outcome,

you have the right to add a statement to your credit report.

- You are entitled to have your credit application reviewed without regard to your sex, marital status, race, age, religion, or receipt of public assistance (receipt of public assistance must be treated as any other income). While this information is sometimes on the application, it cannot be used in the decision.

If you find that one or more of your accounts has been turned over to a debt collection agency, you are protected from abuse. Debt collectors may *not*

- contact you except between the hours of 8 A.M. and 9 P.M.
- contact you at work if your employer does not give permission
- harass or abuse you
- lie to you
- continue to contact you if you request (in writing) that they stop

SUMMARY

Credit is a critical component to achieving financial well-being. Our country's economic growth is dependent upon individuals and businesses using credit to achieve what they otherwise could not. The acquisition and maintenance of credit is a clear signal to employers, landlords, service providers (such as cable and cell phone companies), and other creditors that you are trustworthy.

Once you have established yourself as trustworthy, however, you have the responsibility of checking your credit reports for accuracy, continuing to pay your bills on time, and taking prompt action if you find yourself falling behind in your payments. If you do find yourself in trouble, the best course of action is to act quickly and contact your creditors. Ignoring the problem will never make it go away.

 Test Your Knowledge

1. The major difference between a credit card and a charge card is

    a. you must pay your total balance on a credit card, but you can pay off your charge card balance over time

    b. you must pay your total balance on a charge card, but you can pay off your credit card balance over time

    c. credit cards are made out of plastic, while charge cards are electronic

    d. there is no difference—they are two terms for the same thing

2. A finance charge is

    a. the fee you are charged when you are late with a credit card payment

    b. the fee you are charged just to have a credit card

    c. the fee you are charged for carrying a balance on a credit card

    d. the fee you are charged when you have to replace a lost credit card

3. When a credit card has a fixed APR, it means that

    a. the interest rate on the card can never be changed

    b. the interest rate can be changed, but only when the prime rate changes

    c. the interest rate can change, but the minimum payment stays the same

    d. the interest rate can change, but only if the credit card company gives you sufficient notice

4. What credit card transaction is likely to have the highest interest rate?

    a. cash advance

    b. balance transfer

    c. a regular purchase under your credit limit

    d. an application

5. What is the first step in buying a new car?

    a. figure out how much you can afford in monthly payments

    b. look online to see which cars get the best reviews

    c. find out what your credit score is

    d. look at the ads in your local newspaper to see which dealerships are offering sales

6. An adjustable rate mortgage

    a. has an interest rate that can change at any time during the life of the mortgage

b. has an interest rate that usually is fixed for some period of time then is tied to an index

c. has an interest rate that can only change if the lender gives you notice

d. is a bad idea, no matter what the economic conditions are

7. Which of the following is *not* a way to improve your credit score?

a. only have one type of credit activity, not several different types

b. paying down the amount you owe on open accounts

c. settling a debt for less than you owe and having the creditor report it is paid in full

d. keeping your oldest accounts open and closing some of your newer ones

8. Refund anticipation loans

a. are a convenient way to get a faster refund from the IRS

b. typically have low APRs

c. are not really loans since you are just getting your own money, just faster

d. are loans of your own money for which you pay a high APR

9. Overdraft protection

a. is automatic—you are enrolled as soon as you open an account

    b. is a loan that covers your account if you become overdrawn

    c. will only kick in if you are overdrawn by more than $20

    d. is only activated once per business day, no matter how many times during the day you are overdrawn

10. Under Chapter 7 bankruptcy

    a. all of your debts are erased

    b. some of your debts are erased—you can choose to keep the collateral on a secured loan

    c. your credit report will show a bankruptcy for seven years

    d. you repay your debts under a plan developed by a trustee

Compare your work with the answer key found at the end of the Glossary section.

 Glossary

28/36 rule   A rule that mortgage lenders use to determine the size of a mortgage. Housing costs should make up no more than 28 percent of gross income; total debt should be no more than 36 percent of gross income.

acceleration clause   A clause that may be included in contracts that requires that the loan must be paid off in full if a payment is missed.

adjustable rate mortgage   Mortgage where the interest rate is fixed for a length of time, then is pegged to an index.

annual fee   The fee charged by a credit card company for the use of the card.

annual percentage rate (APR)   The interest rate charged for a loan, expressed on a yearly basis.

application fee   The fee charged by a credit card company to apply for a card.

appreciate   The increase in the value of an asset over time.

balance transfer fee   The fee charged by a credit card company to transfer a balance from an old card to a new one.

balloon loan   Mortgage where the interest rate is fixed for a period of time, after which the entire balance of the loan is due.

bankruptcy   A legal procedure which erases all or part of debt—see Chapter 7 and Chapter 13 bankruptcy, below.

car title loan   A short-term loan that uses a car title as collateral. Interest rates on these loans can be very high.

cash advance   Cash obtained by using a credit card.

cash advance fee   Fee charged by credit card company for getting cash advance.

Chapter 7 bankruptcy   Bankruptcy where most debts are written off, and the debts are no longer owed.

Chapter 13 bankruptcy   Also called wage earner bankruptcy, the debtor repays his/her debts under a repayment plan.

charge card   A card that is used to make purchases, with the full balance due when billed.

collateral   An asset that is security for a loan in case the loan is not repaid.

contactless credit card   A credit card that is activated wirelessly, without swiping it through a reader.

credit card   A card that is used to make purchases by issuing a loan, allowing the customer to pay the balance over time.

Credit CARD Act of 2009   Legislation which increased consumer protections with respect to fees, grace periods, and other aspects of credit card use.

credit counseling agency   An organization that can help consumers set up a budget and manage their debt.

credit limit   The maximum amount an individual is allowed to borrow.

credit report   A history of credit activity, including payments, applications, bankruptcies, and personal information.

credit score   A number ranging from 300 (poor) to 850 (excellent) that denotes credit worthiness.

currency exchange fee   A fee charged by a credit card company for a purchase that requires that U.S. dollars be exchanged for another currency.

debt consolidation loan   A loan that bundles all or most of a consumer's debt into one, replacing several payments into one.

debt-to-income ratio   A fraction composed of the level of outstanding debt divided by gross income.

default   When a debtor fails to make payments on a loan.

default rate   The interest rate that is charged on a credit card if a payment is late or missed.

deficiency clause   A clause that may be in a contract that says that if a debtor fails to repay a loan and the loan's collateral is seized, if a loan balance remains, the debtor still owes it.

depreciate   The reduction in value of an asset over time.

double-cycle billing   A practice used by credit card companies where the company uses both the current balance and the previous balance in computing the finance charge.

Equifax   One of three credit reporting agencies.

equity   The difference between how much an asset is worth and the amount that is owed on it.

Experian   One of the three credit reporting agencies.

Federal Trade Commission (FTC)   Federal agency that oversees consumer rights and protections.

finance charge   The amount of money charged for borrowing money.

fixed interest rate   Interest rate on a credit card that does not change except with 45 day advance notice from the credit card company.

fixed rate mortgage   Mortgage in which the interest rate stays the same for the length of the mortgage.

foreign transaction fee   Fee charged by a credit card company when a purchase is made that requires foreign currency.

garnishment   A legal process by which an employer is required to send a debtor's paychecks (or portion of the paychecks) to a creditor to pay off a loan.

grace period   Period of time when interest is not charged on credit card purchases.

home equity loan   A loan that uses the equity in a house as collateral.

insurance clause   Possible language in a loan contract, requiring the borrower to buy insurance to cover the remainder of the loan in case the borrower dies before the loan is repaid.

interest-only loan   Mortgage where payments in the early years of the loan consist entirely of interest, no payments toward principal.

late fee   The fee charged by a credit card company if a payment is late, nonexistent, or less than the minimum payment.

limited purpose card   A credit card that can only be used at a specific store or business.

mortgage   A loan used for purchasing a house.

multiplier effect   When spending in one sector of the economy spreads to other sectors.

opting in   Choosing to allow a credit card company or bank to cover over-the-limit charges, thus incurring over-the-limit fees.

overdraft protection   A service offered by a financial institution that covers overdrawn accounts, for a fee.

over-the-limit fee   The fee charged by a credit card company if the credit limit is exceeded.

payday loan   A small, short-term loan that is financed by a postdated check. These loans carry very high interest rates.

points   Fees assessed by the lender when making a loan.

previous balance   The amount of a credit card balance that is not paid off from the previous month.

prime rate   The interest rate that banks charge their best customers.

recourse clause   A clause that may be in loan contracts that gives the lender the right to use wage garnishment to collect the balance of a loan if the debtor misses payments.

refinancing   When the original mortgage is replaced by a new one.

refund anticipation loan   A small consumer loan that is secured by a consumer's tax refund.

revolving debt   Debt that does not have a fixed number of payments. Credit card debt is an example.

rewards card   Credit card that includes an incentive for using it, like cash back or airline miles.

secured credit card   A credit card that has collateral attached to it, in the form of a prepaid security deposit.

teaser rate   A low, introductory interest rate on a credit card.

transfer rate   Interest rate that is charged on a credit card balance when it is transferred from an old card to a new card.

TransUnion   One of the three credit reporting agencies.

trustee   A person appointed by the court to oversee a bankruptcy.

unsecured debt   Debt that is not backed by collateral that can be seized in case of nonpayment.

variable interest rate   Credit card interest rate that fluctuates and is pegged to an index.

Answer Key

1. B
2. C
3. D
4. A
5. C
6. B
7. A
8. D
9. B
10. B

Bibliography

Center for Responsible Lending. "Highlights of the New Credit Card Rules: What They Do and Don't Do." Available online. URL: http://www.responsible lending.org/credit-cards/policy-legislation/congress/ Highlights-of-the-New-Credit-Card-Rules-What-They-Do-and-Don-t-Do.html. Accessed May 2010.

Federal Reserve. "Consumer Credit." Federal Reserve Report. Available online. URL: http://www.federal reserve.gov/RELEASES/g19/. Accessed March 2010.

"FICO Credit Scores." Available online. URL: http:// www.money-zine.com/Financial-Planning/Debt-Consolidation/FICO-Credit-Scores/. Accessed May 2010.

Financial Industry Regulatory Authority. "Financial Capability in the United States." Available online. URL: http://www.finra.org/. Accessed February 2011.

Gerson, E., and B. Woolsey. "The History of Credit Cards." Available online. URL: http://www. creditcards.com/credit-card-news/credit-cards-history-1264.php. Accessed April 2010.

"Mortgages and Credit Scores." Available online. URL: http://www.bcsalliance.com/z_creditscore_mortgage. html. Accessed August 2010.

Ostroff, J. "How to Buy New Cars and Avoid Car Dealer Scams." Available online. URL: http://www.car buyingtips.com/car5.htm. Accessed May 2010.

Parrish, L., and U. King. "Phantom Demand: Short Term Due Date Generates Need for Repeat Payday Loans, Accounting for 76 percent of Total Volume." Center for Responsible Lending. Available online. URL: http://www.responsiblelending.org/payday-lending/research-analysis/phantom-demand-final.pdf. Accessed February 2011.

Quester, A., and J. Fox. "Car Title Lenders: Driving Borrowers to Financial Ruin." Center for Responsible Lending. Available online. URL: http://www.responsiblelending.org/other-consumer-loans/car-title-loans/rr008-Car_Title_Lending-0405.pdf. Accessed February 2011.

Richardson, Vanessa. "'Contactless' Credit Cards Spark Concern for Data Privacy." Available online. URL: http://www.creditcards.com/credit-card-news/contactless-credit-cards-data-privacy-1273.php. Accessed April 2010.

Sallie Mae. "How Undergraduate Students Use Credit Cards: Sallie Mae's National Study of Usage Rates and Trends: 2009." Available online. URL: http://www.salliemae.com/NR/rdonlyres/0BD600F1-9377-46EA-AB1F-6061FC763246/10744/SLMCreditCardUsageStudy41309FINAL2.pdf. Accessed February 2011.

Skiba, P., and J. Tobacman. "Do Payday Loans Cause Bankruptcy?" Social Science Research Network. Available online. URL: http://papers.ssrn.com/sol3/papers.cfm?abstract_id=1266215. Accessed February 2011.

Vohwinkle, J. "Beware of the Warning Signs of Too Much Debt." Available online. URL: http://financialplan.about.com/od/creditdebtmanagement/qt/WarningSigns.htm. Accessed May 2010.

"Your FICO Score Is Essential for Getting a Good Mortgage—Today More Than Ever." Available online. URL: http://www.myfico.com/HelpCenter/Mortgages/Buying_a_Home.aspx. Accessed May 2010.

Index